Emerging Science and Technology:

What to Expect in the 2020's, 2030's and Beyond

Roy (Deuce) Andermann Jr

Table of Contents

Preface

The 1989 film Back to the Future II depicted a suite of futuristic technologies in the envisaged year 2015: flying automobiles, hoverboards, video phones, personal drones, mobile payment machines, fingerprint recognition security, and automatic lacing shoes, to name a few. While the movie was markedly prescient regarding their portrayal of technologies like biometric scanning, mobile electronic payment machines and video calling, our post-2015 reality still has not realized the movie's illustration of others, such as hoverboards, automatic lacing shoes and flying automobiles. While director Robert Zemeckis stated that his goal was to make a fun and entertaining rather than a scientifically accurate film, the filmmakers sought the advice of several futurists and consultants to aid in the depictions of the future. Regardless of the underlying motivation behind their representation of 2015, the time-traveling plotline inevitably galvanized movie-goers into pondering and speculating on the future of technology.

Two takeaways can be construed by both comparing and contrasting our current world with that of its portrayal in the movie. Firstly, technology moves extremely quickly. The temporal gap between present and future in the film was only a single generation: 30 years. However, many of the visionary ideas portrayed were indeed realized by 2015. Much of the impetus behind the hastening of modern technological change can be attributed to the invention of the transistor in the 1950's. This technology ushered in an era of low-cost powerful computing that accelerated the pace of innovation and shifted the technological paradigm on a magnitude rivaling the industrial revolution. Underpinned by foundational inventions like the transistor, we routinely use many technologies that would seem extraordinary or alien to a person going to the theatre to see the grand opening of Back to the Future II in 1989.

Secondly, it's difficult to predict which technologies will be realized in a given timeframe. To paraphrase Isaac Newton (and by reference, 12th century French philosopher Bernard of Chartres), we see further by standing on the shoulders of giants. That is, technological discovery hinges on building upon previous discoveries of our ancestors. This is particularly evident in the innovation of keystone technologies that open the door to other technologies. The aforementioned invention of the seemingly insipid transistor that engendered massive innovation in computing is one such example. Other examples of keystone technologies of the past are the internal combustion engine and the plow. While the technological revolution permitted by the engine is clear, the plow's impact is more indirect. Pre-plow, nearly all villagers in towns or communes were tasked with gathering or growing food to survive. The invention of the plow permitted the division of labor. Post-plow, since only a small fraction of the village members were necessary to produce enough food to supply the entire village, other members were now able to take a step back, think, and innovate. People could now develop or specialize in rudimentary carpentry, tool-making, metallurgy, medicine, and other fields. Two yet-unrealized keystone technologies include room-temperature superconductivity and high-precision graphene production. Since many futuristic technologies rely on our mastery these two technologies, predictions of when we may realize fanciful widgets of the 2060's or 2070's vary wildly because their development is contingent upon prior innovation of other technologies that themselves are subject to unstable funding and varied temporal estimates of development and commercial rollout.

So where does this leave us in our quest to discover realistic estimates of what the future holds regarding both newly invented emerging technologies as well as those not yet realized? Well, since many technologies that will be discussed here depend on unresolved science, estimates will vary wildly. These estimates can swing even further if the holder of the opinion has an unconscious or conscious bias. For instance, startup tech CEOs' prospects for acquiring funding hinges upon the viability of the company's technology and timeline projections for completion of a marketable prototype. These CEOs are under enormous pressure to be optimistic with their predictions of the timeframe for realization of their technologies. Likewise, news outlets desperate for views or clicks are also incentivized to be overly optimistic or economical with the truth regarding cutting edge technologies to draw in and retain more viewers or readers. On the other side of the coin, stakeholders with an interest in maintaining the status quo, often large corporations profiting from a technology at risk of disruption, will have an interest in downplaying new disruptive technologies and estimating a long timeframe until the technology will be realized to calm the shareholders. Thus it's imperative to both examine multiple sources and to dive down into the science to get a comprehensive outlook on what to expect regarding a given technology.

Each of the upcoming entries includes two quick briefs that precede the main article: first is the status of the science or technology as of 2020, and second is an estimate of what we can expect from the research or technology moving in the future, including time estimates or ranges. The articles seek to both explicate the underlying science and, if applicable, to probe what hurdles hinder wide-scale commercial implementation of the technologies, whether they be technological, economical, ethical, or regulatory.

Sector 1: Energy

<u>Energy Topic 1: Fusion Power</u>

Status of the technology: Several research teams around the world have succeeded in creating fusion. However, no team has yet been able to generate more power output than the amount of power put into the system. Highest yet achieved was the Joint European Torus (JET) reactor in England in 1997, where output power was 67% of the energy put into the system.

What to expect: Don't hold your breath. Much of the future of fusion hinges on what happens when the ITER, the International Thermonuclear Experimental Reactor, in France commences operation in 2025. The reactor is expected to realize an energy gain of 10 (10 times higher energy output than the energy input). If everything with ITER goes well, then a follow-up power station called DEMO will be constructed, which claims it would be operational and generating power by 2033. However, that seems massively optimistic. Realistically I wouldn't expect commercial fusion power before 2050.

A variety of renewable and clean energies are being developed as a successor to fossil fuels. While solar and wind power show some promise, it's imperative that scientists develop concomitant battery technology beyond what is currently available to store energy for whenever these technologies aren't producing power. Without powerful, sophisticated and yet unrealized batteries, solar and wind power will remain nothing more than a supplement to more stable energy technologies. Further, with solar and wind it's difficult to match power generation with temporal and spatial swings in demand; power production is almost entirely at the mercy of the weather, regardless of downstream demand. Thus, fusion power stands as one of the cleanest and most viable alternatives to fossil fuels. Fusion plants would be able to connect directly to the existing electrical grid and could use existing infrastructure that was built for coal, gas or nuclear fission plants. Fusion would also allow operators to directly control power generation to keep up with swings in demand.

For a quick summary of the science, a fusion reaction occurs when two small atomic nuclei are combined to form a larger nucleus. The sum of the mass of the two smaller nuclei is slightly higher than the mass of the single larger nucleus, and that disparity in mass is released as energy as described by Einstein's famous $E=mc^2$ equation. This reaction can only occur when the two small nuclei are able to approach one another close enough for the short-ranged attractive nuclear force to overcome longer-range electrostatic repulsive forces. As an analogy, you can think of this like trying to force two "like" magnets to touch. They'll greatly resist getting close to one another, no matter how hard you push (analogous to the longer-acting electrostatic forces). But if you can somehow put in enough energy to get the magnets to touch, a much stronger but very short-range force will lock them together (analogous to the nuclear force). What this means for nuclear fusion is that it takes an incredible amount of energy input to get the atoms close enough for the nuclear force to lock the atoms together. Consequently, fusion reactors require great upfront capital in addition to high ongoing operating expenses to run experiments safely and on any appreciable scale.

The scientific community likes to joke that fusion power is always just 20 years away. The joke isn't completely unfounded; fusion power truly does seem to have been just out of scientific reach for about 70 years at this point. Fusion was first experimentally demonstrated nearly a century ago via particle accelerator in the late 1920's in England. Since then, research has never completely ossified; incremental progress has been made throughout the decades and commercially viable fusion has always seemed probable within the upcoming few decades. It remains to be seen whether the ITER reactor in France will break the curse and prove, once and for all, that positive energy gain and commercially viable fusion are possible.

The temperature and pressure conditions in a reactor must be extreme for fusion to occur. The reactants, usually deuterium and tritium as will be explicated below, must be in plasma phase, which means their nuclei have been stripped of their electrons. In the core of stars, the immense pressure from gravity produces heat and creates such a plasma. Within the plasma, two hydrogen atoms are typically combined into a helium atom, releasing light and heat. These are the extreme temperature and pressure conditions that fusion scientists seek to recreate on Earth.

Two key methods to form plasmas and to reach temperatures high enough to fuse hydrogen or hydrogen isotopes include magnetic confinement and inertial confinement. **Magnetic confinement** reactors use a magnetic field created by superconducting electromagnets to squeeze plasma in a central chamber where the reaction takes place. The plasma ions are charged and thus can be controlled by the magnets. **Inertial confinement**, on the other hand, uses powerful laser pulses to heat deuterium and tritium fuel, imploding it to initiate fusion. This method takes incredible precision and timing for the lasers to properly heat the fuel enough to initiate fusion.

While magnetic confinement and inertial confinement are the two most studied methods and generally exhibit the most promise, there are several other methods, as well as several variations on and subcategories of these two methods being explored. One alternative is magnetized target fusion, which is essentially a combination of the aforementioned magnetic confinement and inertial confinement. Inertial electrostatic confinement and fusors are both methods that use electrical fields to initiate fusion. In short, scientists have a suite of setups and methods at their disposal, usually involving some combination of electric currents, electric fields, magnetic fields, and lasers.

So, we have the technology to heat hydrogen to higher than the temperature of the sun and can cause fusion to occur. We can also keep the plasma contained, so why don't we have fusion power plants yet? The issue keeping us from realizing commercial fusion power is a constant called Q. Q is the **energy gain**, which is the ratio of energy in versus energy out. Thus far, scientists have not been able to achieve the elusive break-even point, the Q of 1, which would mean that we receive the same power output as input. It's difficult and expensive to achieve the required pressure and temperature combination to initiate fusion, so it requires a very large electricity input. The highest Q achieved thus far is 0.67 from the JET reactor, a magnetic confinement reactor, in England back in 1999. This reactor has also reached temperatures of over 200 million degrees Celsius. As impressive as this is, electrical power plants are only viable if they make more electricity than they consume. Even a Q slightly higher than 1 wouldn't be economically viable, as the marginal profits wouldn't be sufficient to offset capital and operating costs. Commercialization is unlikely to occur until the technology improves to the point that reactors can realize a Q of 10 or more.

Fusion experiments require a lot of time to set up, and after each test reactors must often be abandoned for a few months to years before the radioactive equipment is safe to use again. Thus it's not uncommon for several years to pass between tests. Largely for these reasons the current world record Q was achieved so long ago, in 1999. However, we can expect the record to be broken soon. The goal for the international megaproject ITER is to have an energy output 10 times higher than input. ITER is a magnetic confinement reactor planned to start up in 2025 and it's only a scientific venture to demonstrate the scientific and technological feasibility of fusion power; it won't directly power any grid. ITER is not a government project; rather, it's a multi-government project so delays and budget overruns are a near certainty. If ITER does indeed achieve or surpass its goals, a fusion power plant called DEMO (DEMOnstration Power Station) will be constructed with hopes to use fusion to power the grid around 2030 to 2050.

The "easiest" achievable fusion reaction is to combine deuterium and tritium to form helium plus a spare neutron. Ultimately, there are a suite of possible fusion reactions, combining various isotopes of small elements together, such as protium, deuterium, tritium (three different isotopes of hydrogen), helium, lithium, and boron. Some of these reactions can produce much more energy than the deuterium-tritium reaction, but the deuterium-tritium reaction has the lowest energy threshold. To elucidate, reactions other than deuterium-tritium require more extreme temperature and pressure conditions. Once the deuterium-tritium reaction proves the feasibility of the underlying science, scientists may move on to more sophisticated reactions such as proton-boron fusion, which results in less dangerous neutron radiation and would be more amenable to directly generating harnessable power.

The deuterium-tritium reaction does have its perks though. Deuterium is relatively easy to procure since it's a natural isotope of hydrogen. About one in 6,500 hydrogen atoms in seawater is deuterium, which means that seawater could be used as fuel. Tritium can be produced on site at the fusion facility by irradiating lithium.

In sum, generating fusion is not very difficult for modern technology and equipment; it's just extremely expensive, turns equipment dangerously radioactive, and it's been challenging to conduct experiments in a manner that results in a positive energy gain. We still don't know for sure if fusion will ever achieve a positive energy gain, but computer simulations suggest that it's quite possible, if not probable. Assuming scientists can achieve economically viable fusion, another hurdle to commercialization would be the durability of the system. Neutrons released during fusion degrade materials in the walls of the reactor, so advancements in materials science would be necessary to increase the lifespan of the reactors. We'll have to cross that bridge once we come to it – the first step is to surpass that elusive Q of 1.

As they say, fusion power is just 20 years away.

Energy Topic 2: Thorium Nuclear Power

Status of the technology: Proven technology. The Oak Ridge National Laboratory in Tennessee, USA created a working prototype thorium reactor in the 1960's. However, no thorium reactors are currently online.

What to expect: Japan, China and a suite of European countries have demonstrated interest in launching collaborative experimental thorium reactors in the medium term, around 10 or 15 years into the future. We can expect several experimental reactors coming online between 2030 and 2040. Widescale electrical power from thorium would come a decade or so later, pending all goes well with the experimental reactors.

At present, fission nuclear power is dominated by power plants primarily using the element uranium, but it has a strong challenger: thorium. Thorium is 3 times more abundant than uranium in earth's crust and its ore is more concentrated, making mining more commercially viable and saving energy during processing and purification. Thorium doesn't need to be enriched before use like uranium does, and one ton of thorium can produce as much energy as 35 tons of uranium or 4 million tons of coal. Thorium creates less than 1% of the nuclear waste that uranium produces. Thorium reactors are more efficient than uranium reactors, and since thorium would be in liquid form while producing power, it could be refueled while operating, which results in less down time. The liquid thorium would act as both the fuel and the coolant, meaning that it could self-regulate and slow the reaction down if the temperature gets too high. Thorium reactors could also be constructed in a manner that would render them incapable of having a meltdown.

This all sounds too good to be true. Why aren't we using thorium? As it turns out, the reason uranium has achieved dominance is chiefly geopolitical rather than scientific or technological. That being said, thorium also does have its own drawbacks, which we'll get to later.

Pivotal funding decisions for research into nuclear power occurred in the 1960s. At this point in history, the key prospective nuclear powers were deep into a cold war. The thorium fuel cycle involves converting thorium into uranium <u>233</u> to use as fuel, which is terrible for making nuclear bombs. Typical uranium reactors utilize uranium <u>235</u> for fuel, which is much better for making bombs. The governments of the superpowers faced a choice: fund research into thorium reactors which would only contribute to the energy revolution, or fund research into uranium reactors which could contribute to both the energy revolution as well as nuclear bomb development. As I'm sure you've already predicted, during the height of the cold war uranium research received virtually all available funding whereas thorium research was cast aside. With this cash infusion, uranium fission and power became so widely researched and meticulously characterized that uranium plants ultimately became the industry standard that continued for decades.

Nowadays, thorium's lack of ability to be fabricated into bombs is an attractive quality rather than dissuasive. The pros delineated in the opening paragraph have engendered renewed interest in pursuing research into thorium reactors. However, pursual of thorium power faces economic headwinds: uranium has been so extensively researched and utilized that it's simple and cheap (relatively speaking) to set up a cookie-cutter uranium plant; the parameters and kinks have already been worked out through decades of research, trial and error. Pursuing thorium power is a whole new endeavor with many unknowns and a higher price tag.

Uranium is **fissile**, which means that it will split and undergo fission when hit by a neutron. In contrast, thorium is **fertile**, which means that it will absorb neutrons to become a fissile material.

This means that thorium is much safer, and a thorium reaction can't run away in an implacable positive feedback loop the way a uranium reaction can. A helper material like uranium or plutonium must be added to the reactor to convert thorium into uranium to get the reaction to go critical. In addition, liquid thorium reactors typically have a freeze plug at the bottom. If the reaction gets too hot it will melt the plug and the thorium will drain out of the reactor and away from the source of neutrons, i.e. the uranium or plutonium initiator. This makes it incredibly unlikely, or even nearly impossible, to have a catastrophic accident in a thorium reactor.

Thorium reactors have a simpler construction than uranium reactors. A thorium reactor could be comprised of not much more than a vat since the reactant would be in liquid form. There would be no need for fuel cells or rods. Uranium reactors, in contrast, use solid uranium dioxide fuel pellets that are inserted into rods that must be carefully managed to maintain temperature within a pre-set parameter range.

Liquid Fluoride Thorium Reactors (LFTRs) use molten salt coolant which allows for higher operating temperatures and less pressure than uranium reactors. Since the thorium plants would not need to be pressurized, they have smaller containment requirements. This would allow the possibility of constructing smaller decentralized plants in contrast to the few, large uranium plants typical of operations today.

Thorium power is not without downsides. First off, thorium reactors are still in the research stage since they haven't been historically funded well. Since only limited practical research has been undertaken to date, we simply don't know what new downsides may manifest once functional reactors are built. The most salient and immediate downside is the challenge of finding materials that can resist the highly corrosive molten salts of a thorium reactor. These reactors would experience quick material degradation that would require more maintenance than uranium reactors. However, once more initial capital has been invested into thorium research and scientists learn more granular information about the pros and cons, it is highly likely that it will prove to be a greener, safer, cheaper, more efficient technology when compared to uranium power.

Public apathy toward thorium power is an encumbrance to receiving governmental funding for thorium research. Thorium power isn't as sexy as most other alternative energy technologies like wind, solar, or artificial photosynthesis so it receives less media attention. However, it's much more reliable than these technologies and can meet the needs of the world's energy consumption several times over.

Speaking of artificial photosynthesis...

Energy Topic 3: Artificial photosynthesis

Status of the technology: Proof of concept completed for several different artificial photosynthesis methods. Low efficiency in energy production and high price due to the requirement of gold or platinum-group metal catalysts remain as hurdles to commercialization.

What to expect: Alternatives to expensive metal catalysts have been tested with initial success, so we could reasonably expect an initial rollout of artificial photosynthesis-derived fuels before 2030.

Humanity is currently experiencing a paradigm shift in energy production and use. A suite of renewable energy technologies are being developed as energies of the future, with wind and solar being two frontrunners. However, these two technologies have major downsides: they only work when conditions are windy or sunny, respectively, and it's very difficult to distribute and store the energy they produce. Parallel advances in energy storage technology will be a necessity for these technologies to gain widespread use.

If not for their atmosphere-altering effects and finiteness of supply, chemical fuels such as gasoline would be nearly perfect energy sources. They're extremely energy dense, highly transportable, and don't rely on being tied to an electrical grid. Fossil fuels are in essence stored sunlight, since photosynthetic organisms like plants use light as the energy source to fix the carbon from the air into biomass, and then die and turn into fuels. One division of clean energy research seeks to mimic this process by producing chemical biofuels such as corn-derived ethanol. The problem with this method is that the process of producing biofuels is very inefficient. After accounting for the application of fertilizers and the energy used to grow, harvest, transport and process the corn, the net benefit of the resulting biofuel over fossil fuels is marginal at best. These fuels aren't nearly as "clean" as marketing campaigns make them seem.

A much more efficient way to harness the power of the sun to produce chemical fuels exists: **artificial photosynthesis**. This technology has generated a new category of fuel termed "solar fuels" and aims to directly use sunlight to produce fuels from only water and air, much like a plant does. The term artificial photosynthesis is broader than it may at first seem, as it encompasses any technologies that transduce solar energy to chemical energy; a suite of disparate emerging technologies fit this description. Sugar, the product of plant photosynthesis, need not be the product. In fact, since sugar is a large and complex molecule, most efforts aim to produce simpler fuels like hydrogen, oxygen, methane, formic acid, or butane. The unifying goal is to efficiently fix carbon dioxide gas from the air into higher-energy liquid or solid compounds that can be used as fuel or food.

Artificial photosynthesis methods can be separated into two classes: direct and indirect. Direct methods harness the energy of sunlight to produce a fuel without any intermediary energy conversions. Indirect methods, by contrast, convert solar energy to electricity first and then use the electricity to synthesize a fuel. Indirect methods often focus on using the electricity to split water into hydrogen and oxygen, which themselves are fuels that can be burned. In general, direct methods are more efficient but are also more difficult to create and implement.

Here is a quick survey of several methods being researched and tested for using sunlight to create organic, hydrogen or oxygen fuels; it is by no means inclusive of all technologies:

1) Direct method – using metal catalysts bound to a silica to convert carbon dioxide to formic acid. The formic acid could then be harvested and either used as-is as a fuel,

preservative, or antibacterial, or converted to other compounds.

2) Direct method – using the natural enzyme NADPH which is found in plants and animals. NADPH is a key enzyme in creating energy within cells and is recyclable in its natural cycle in organisms. This technology is very new but it shows promise. It could be used to transport electrons back and forth to produce fuels while it oscillates between its oxidized and non-oxidized forms NADP+ and NADPH. Proof of concept has been demonstrated when pairing this enzyme with artificial ruthenium-based complexes.

3) Indirect method. Solar panels or a photosensitive electrode converts light into electric current. The current then splits water into hydrogen and oxygen. The hydrogen and oxygen can be used as fuel.

4) Indirect method. Genetically engineer algae to produce fuels like hydrogen, methanol, butanol, and hexanol. This method has already succeeded in large-scale experiments. There are several ways to accomplish this, but a popular method is to split carbon dioxide and water into carbon monoxide and hydrogen, then bubble these into a tank containing the bacteria, which convert these reactive molecules into fuels.

Two main hurdles hinder commercialization of most of these technologies:

1) Sensitivity to carbon dioxide. The carbon dioxide concentration in the ambient atmosphere is less than one-tenth of one percent. For many technologies that seek to use carbon dioxide as a reactant, results typically only manifest when the concentration is raised significantly above normal atmospheric levels. Scientists have not been able to match plants' ability to fix carbon dioxide from a gas to a solid or liquid at ambient concentrations yet. Many

experiments and proofs-of-concept in the field utilized air that had been previously concentrated to higher than atmospheric concentrations, but any viable commercial rollout would necessarily require that the technology work at atmospheric concentrations.

2) Price. Expensive metals like platinum and gold are the most effective catalysts to split water. In addition to better catalytic activity, gold nanoparticles do not break down like other metals do, so they have higher longevity. Though these work great, the cost would impede wide-spread implementation. A few research groups have had success splitting water with cheaper materials like copper, nickel, molybdenum and zinc, so it's likely that the field will be able to transition away from expensive catalysts in the future.

The future of artificial photosynthesis is bright. Since liquid fuels can be stored for later use, they have an inherent advantage over almost all other clean energy sources and still may see implementation even if other renewable energies dominate in generating electrical power for the grid. The most promising technology at the moment is likely the conversion of solar energy into hydrogen via water-splitting assisted by photosemiconductor catalysts. Since very large quantities of hydrogen can be produced using this method, fuel for hydrogen engines could become very affordable in the near future.

Energy Topic 4: Ocean Thermal Energy Conversion

Status of the technology: Proven technology. Positive net energy output has been achieved on several occasions. Several experimental OTEC plants are currently active.

What to expect: Several countries such as the US, Japan and India plan to build more experimental OTEC plants in the near future. Soon, plants will likely start connecting to grids and contributing to the energy needs of coastal populations near warm ocean surface waters, which are conducive to the technology. We can also expect plants to be built on small tropical island nations where traditional energy is prohibitively expensive.

While solar and wind energy dominate the renewable energy conversation, a lesser known technology called Ocean Thermal Energy Conversion (OTEC) may be a more viable option for humanity's future clean energy needs. This technology has the potential to provide the total energy needs of the planet many times over, and with no carbon release.

Sunlight reaching the ocean is attenuated as it travels deeper and deeper through the water. The region from the surface to 200 meters deep is the bright area where photosynthetic organisms dwell. From 200 meters to 1,000 meters sunlight rapidly diminishes with depth, and below 1,000 meters the ocean is virtually completely black. This gradient of energy input in the water column results in a corresponding temperature gradient; surface waters are generally around 20°C (36°F) warmer than the deeper waters. This temperature disparity combined with the enormous mass of the ocean provides an opportunity to generate huge amounts of electricity.

The principle behind Ocean Thermal Energy Conversion is very similar to, but opposite of, the cooling system of a refrigerator or automotive air conditioning systems. Both systems exploit the phase changes of a refrigerant (back and forth between liquid and gas) in a closed-pipe system, but refrigerators use energy to create a heat differential whereas OTEC uses a heat differential to create energy.

For ease of discussion, we'll assume that the refrigerant used in the pipes of our example OTEC system below is ammonia, though most substances with a boiling point between that of cold, deep seawater ($\approx$5°C or 41°F) and warm, surface seawater ($\approx$25°C or 77°F in tropics) would suffice. Propane and freon refrigerants like R-134a are popular alternatives to ammonia.

The system contains:

1) An evaporator to boil the liquid ammonia into a gas
2) A turbine whose blades are spun by the boiled ammonia to generate electricity via an attached generator
3) A condenser to condense the gaseous ammonia back to a liquid
4) Pumps to move the ammonia around the system
5) Pipes. Lots and lots of pipes

The cold seawater is pumped from around 1,000 meters deep to near the surface to run the condenser. The condenser acts as a heat exchanger, bringing hot ammonia in the pipes and the cold seawater right next to each other but doesn't let them mix. The hot gaseous ammonia loses heat in the condenser and condenses into a liquid. In a similar vein, the warm surface seawater runs the evaporator. The liquid ammonia is brought into proximity with warm seawater, which boils the ammonia. The ammonia vapor then goes on to turn the turbine. Boiling the ammonia increases its pressure, which gives it transferrable energy to spin the turbine much like boiled water, steam, turns turbines in conventional coal-fired power plants and nuclear plants. The turbine is connected to a generator, which creates power to provide electricity directly to the grid.

And that's it. From a theoretical perspective, OTEC systems are quite simple. It uses hot and cold seawater to manipulate phase changes in a refrigerant which can produce electricity. Since hot and cold seawater are a virtually infinite resource, as long as the amount of electricity produced surpasses what is needed to run the pumps and auxiliary equipment, the system can create essentially free electricity (not counting capital and maintenance costs, of course).

The temperature difference between surface water and deeper water becomes increasingly muted as one travels in latitude away from the equator, chiefly due to the drop in surface temperature. Near the arctic the temperature gradient almost completely disappears. Thus, OTEC plants are mostly viable only in the tropics, where the temperature difference between surface water and 1,000 meter deep water can be as high as 25°C (45°F). As a natural consequence, proposed OTEC projects concentrate on the Caribbean, Indian Ocean, Hawaii, and South China Sea areas. Special interest has focused on installing OTEC plants to serve the needs of small tropical islands without many other natural energy resources, like Kiribati, Nauru, and the Maldives. Building the first generation of OTEC plants in these areas may be the most economically sound option since competing sources of electricity are very expensive.

OTEC plants can be built on land, anchored at sea to the continental shelf, or as floating platforms. While most concept OTECs focus on the sea platform route, some active experiments such as the Makai OTEC plant in Hawaii have found success pumping both warm and cold seawater on shore for non-mobile land-based operations.

OTEC plants have been built periodically over the past few decades, mainly focused in Japan and Hawaii. Japan built an OTEC plant in the 1980s on the island of Nauru that had a positive net power output and connected to the grid rather than being purely experimental. Hawaii's aforementioned Makai OTEC plant also generates positive energy. These two countries will likely be joined by India as the key players moving forward.

Pumping cold water from the depths to the surface could offer several auxiliary benefits besides its contribution to power generation, including:

1) Open-system OTEC plants (different layout and operations than the closed-system style that we discussed here, but the underlying thermodynamic principles remain the same) would produce desalinated water as a byproduct that could be used for drinking or irrigation.
2) Deep water is typically rich in nutrients. This water could be utilized for raising fish, seaweed, oysters, or other marine organisms for commercial use via aquaculture.
3) Deep water also typically contains minerals such as rare earth elements, lithium, uranium, and precious metals. Mineral extraction of deep waters has previously been economically unviable, but if the water is already being pumped to the surface for another use, resource extraction could become economically worthwhile.
4) The cool water could be used in cooling towers and apparatuses for industrial plants. Many types of heavy industrial plants intake seawater or river water to cool their equipment. The availability of 5°C water would increase the efficiency of cooling equipment over ambient or surface seawater.

The information thus far makes this technology seem like a no-brainer. However, it does have its downsides. While it's true that the energy an OTEC plant produces would be essentially free, it requires a great deal of upfront capital to construct the system, which dissuades risk-averse investors. A second downside is microbial fouling. Since the evaporator and condenser will be open to raw seawater, it can't be treated with anti-algals. Even a tiny layer of biofilm less than a millimeter thick on the evaporator or condenser can reduce heat transfer efficiency by 50% or more. More extreme fouling can block flows entirely. Thus, the piping requires active maintenance to remain efficient. Speaking of efficient, low efficiency is a third downside. Due to the low temperature difference between surface water and deep water, thermal efficiency of the OTEC plants is quite low, usually around 3-4%. For comparison, gas engines are around 25% efficient and coal plants and diesel engines about 50%.

At present, the majority of the energy created by OTEC systems is needed to push the refrigerant and seawater around the system and to run ancillary devices. However, efficiency can be improved by utilizing cleverly designed geometries that take advantage of surface currents to create pressure differentials to passively draw water into the system. For instance, the Gulf Stream's predictable and directionally stable northward flow could be exploited by creating a passive inlet for surface water.

In sum, OTEC captures energy from the differential heating of layers of the ocean by the Sun. Thus, the technology indirectly harnesses the energy from sunlight and can be thought of as a more stable and predictable type of solar renewable energy when compared to traditional solar cells. However, due to the high initial cost, OTEC electricity would likely need to be subsidized, at least in its early days, if it is to compete with the bigger players for the future of energy.

Energy Topic 5: Smart grid

Status of the technology: Several smart grid deployments have already been rolled out in countries around the world such as Italy, Australia, Portugal, Canada and several US states.

What to expect: The smart grid is still years away in most places. Significant capital investment will be required to modernize most aging grids. Many regions of industrialized countries can expect a smarter grid by 2030.

The electric grids of most countries were originally designed for little demand per household. Until only the last few decades, most houses had lights, radios and a few appliances but not much more. At this stage in history, information on electricity usage was transferred one way: from the consumer to the utility company, who analyzed the customer's energy usage and sent a bill. With the recent increase in energy demand from consumers due to smart appliances, computers, electric vehicles, and other modern electric amenities, it's often difficult for the grid to keep up. The smart grid is a modernization of the old grid that includes a suite of sensors and technologies intended to address the challenges of efficiently supplying electricity to the consumers that carry an ever-increasing energy demand. The new grids would permit a two-way dialogue where both electricity and information can travel both ways, from the consumer to utility company and vice versa. As such, the smart grid isn't just one technology, but rather an idea. The increased transfer of knowledge and data should allow production and consumption to increase in efficiency and reliability and attenuate peaks and troughs in both electrical demand and generation.

Step 1 in building a smart grid is to increase information communication. Both sides, the consumer and the utility company, must apprise one another with real-time information for any benefits and cost-reductions to be realized. This requires capital investment into sensors that analyze electrical current and quality, smart electrical boxes installed at homes that can relay energy usage information to the utility company and receive information back, and rollouts of information technology programs to analyze the data in real time to facilitate decision making. The sensors and software that would be added to the existing grid would give both the utility companies and individuals information that would allow them to react accordingly. Users could lower usage whenever demand is highest and electricity is most expensive, whereas grid operators could visualize demand and adjust power output in real time as they receive information concerning demand.

The data from the new sensors would allow the utility company to locate power failures instantly and automatically reroute electricity or avoid overheating power lines. The smart grid would instantly re-route the power around the problem, causing minimal disruption for consumers. At present, powerline damages typically require electricity to be manually shifted to re-route power.

The smart grid allows for incorporation of new renewable energies as well as for high-demand electrical implements like electric vehicles. Consumers who own their own electricity-producing assets like solar panels could sell their energy onto the grid. Energy created during peak hours will command a premium over energy created during off-hours. As more homeowners install clean energy production technologies, the grid will shift from a centralized entity to a distributed grid with power generation shared across the network. However, adding feed-in points to allow power from small producers to enter the system and distribute the input is not a trivial matter; this will require additional investment as part of the smart grid rollout plans.

Utility companies' approach of keeping backup power plants operational and ready to inject power into the system to cover peak demand is often the most expensive part of a consumer's power bill. Thus, heavy motivation exists to smoothen the peaks in demand, even if total daily or weekly energy consumption remains unchanged. One method to aid in leveling demand is to implement smart appliances and devices such as washing machines and dryers that can talk to the grid and adjust their run schedule to when demand is lowest. Consumers will be able to designate certain devices as low priority, and by running these appliances during off-hours electricity production can be more evenly produced throughout the day. The billed cost of power could be time-dependent to offer a discount during off-peak hours and incentivize customers to lower energy usage during peak times by instead operating devices during lulls in demand. This demand-side management would result in a direct economic benefit to consumers of operating devices during non-peak hours.

An alternative to aid in leveling peaks involves storing energy created during off-peak hours in batteries to discharge during peak hours. While this sounds great in theory, an array of batteries large enough to have a tangible supply-side impact would be incredibly expensive. Battery technology leaves a lot to be desired and is one of the key factors slowing the rollout of renewable energies like solar and wind. Ongoing research into fluoride-ion batteries, solid-state batteries, and graphene-based batteries and capacitors may change the game, but as of now it's prohibitively expensive to store such a large amount of energy.

Private individuals releasing masses of granular data or metadata to external parties raises serious issues concerning privacy. Much of the infrastructure for the smart grid relies on electronics in houses being monitored for use. The garnered data opens up the possibility of social abuse of the information going to the utility companies as well as concerns regarding censorship. Some smart grid proposals include the ability for utility companies to use kill switches to control household implements in the event of a power overload. These same switches could theoretically be used to selectively cut power to consumers for political or other purposes. Yet another concern is the increased risk of cyberattacks since much of the information transfer to and from the utility company will be done online. Lastly, the variable rates for electrical usage could be manipulated by the utility company to take financial advantage of the consumer.

The rollout of smart grids will be a gradual process occurring over the next few decades. China plans to begin construction of their upgraded grid in the early 2020's. The United States is injecting money from fiscal stimulus packages into smart grid construction in various states. Significant initiatives are also being launched in Japan, Europe, Australia and South Korea. Altogether, there are around 100 pilot projects underway worldwide. Many people will likely notice a gradual rather than saltatory shift towards the new grid.

Sector 2: Space

<u>Space Topic 1: Terraforming</u>

Status of the technology: Relegated to science fiction for the foreseeable future.

What to expect: Undertaking terraforming is far beyond our current capabilities. The hindrance is primarily due to massive scale and insurmountable cost of any terraforming project. However, a fair portion of the underlying techniques are available with current technology.

Terraforming is the process of transforming a hostile environment into one that can support human life. A staple of science fiction, many astronomical bodies have been targets of speculation on the plausibility of terraforming. While some terraforming techniques are fantastical, many techniques are surprisingly within our current technological capabilities. However, the economic burden associated with terraforming ensures that terraforming will remain in the realm of science fiction for decades, if not centuries. With costs ranging from trillions to quadrillions or more US dollars, the economics are far beyond any government or private entity's willingness to spend. In fact, even a collective pooling of all of humanity's current resources is not sufficient to undertake a large-scale terraforming project.

That being said, let's not let the economic unviability dissuade us from diving into the science. If humans were to terraform a planetary body it would likely be one within our own solar system.

Top candidates include Mercury, Venus, the Moon, Mars, Jupiter's moons Ganymede, Callisto and Europa, or Saturn's moons Enceladus and Titan. The ultimate goal is to engineer a planet or moon to "feel" similar to Earth by nudging astronomical and environmental parameters until they become earth-like. Parameters to be adjusted include gravity, temperature, air pressure, water and water vapor, day length, year length, air composition, presence of soil, and amount of radiation reaching the surface. The three most important parameters are temperature, atmosphere and water; all others are secondary, since failure to adjust these three parameters to a level similar to Earth's will not render the planet habitable.

Each of the aforementioned candidate celestial bodies has its own particular set of pros and cons. Some atmospheres, like that of Venus or Titan, are thicker than the Earth's, whereas most others are thinner. Venus' and Mars' atmospheres contain mostly carbon dioxide, but Titan's is mostly nitrogen. Each planet or moon has a unique set of attributes which means that any potential terraforming project must be uniquely specialized and targeted to that particular body. There is no one-size-fits-all solution.

Radiation

Earth's magnetosphere blocks or attenuates cosmic and solar radiation before it reaches Earth's surface. High levels of ionizing radiation can damage DNA and are incompatible with long-term survival, so terraforming of a planet without a magnetosphere must contain some method to protect the inhabitants from radiation. One proposal is to use nuclear warheads to jumpstart a rocky planet's core to generate its own spin and develop a magnetosphere. While attractive in theory, the cost and logistics of getting nukes near the core quickly render this infeasible. A less sophisticated alternative option is to purposely litter the atmosphere with material that would deflect away radiation. A third approach to generate a magnetosphere is to employ solar powered satellites around the planet that generate magnetic fields. With the current level of knowledge and technology, this artificial magnetosphere solution would be our best bet for most terraforming projects, especially with the optimistic research on superconductors.

Atmosphere

Few planets or celestial bodies have an atmosphere comparably thick to Earth's. The atmospheres of most candidates are very thin, but Venus is an outlier with an atmosphere around 100 times denser than Earth's. Though Venus' atmosphere is thick, its nitrogen composition is only about 3.5%, which results in the planet having a total level of nitrogen that's higher but somewhat similar to Earth's concentration, which is an attractive quality. Furthermore, the gravity on Venus is about the same as Earth's and the planet receives plenty of sunlight; it's superior to candidates like Mars in several respects. Proposals to rarefy Venus' 96% carbon dioxide atmosphere usually employ chemistry rather than physical removal of the atmosphere. Theories include seeding the planet with bacteria that would consume the carbon dioxide, dousing the planet with hydrogen to react with the carbon dioxide to produce graphite, or bombarding it with magnesium or calcium to stimulate formation of carbon-containing rock to sequester the gaseous carbon dioxide into the ground.

At the other end of the spectrum we have Mars, whose atmosphere is about 1% as thick as Earth's. Interestingly, like Venus its atmosphere is also comprised of about 96% carbon dioxide. Mars has no magnetosphere and would require a much denser atmosphere to support life. If we provide Mars with a magnetosphere by employing one of the technologies introduced earlier, it would not only protect organisms from radiation, but would also decrease the amount of its atmosphere that's stripped away by solar wind. The atmosphere would slowly thicken if we set up a force field around the planet, as gas is constantly leaking out of Mars' crust. However, while the science is sound, the timescale renders relying purely on capturing outgas to form a habitable atmosphere impractical.

Alternatively, we could thicken Mars' atmosphere by utilizing the greenhouse effect -- humans are already great at warming planets using this technique. Adding almost any gas could aid the process, such as methane, carbon dioxide, ammonia or nitrogen. Scientists could kill two birds with one stone by transporting nitrogen from Venus to Mars. As mentioned earlier, while Venus' atmosphere has only 3.5% nitrogen compared to Earth's 70%, Venus' dense atmosphere results in an overall higher nitrogen concentration than Earth, and thus we could remove some of Venus' nitrogen to get a more Earthlike atmosphere on that planet. Methane could be mined directly from rocks on Mars, and water vapor and carbon dioxide are both also slowly being released from rocks into the atmosphere. Ammonia and hydrocarbons could be harvested from moons in the outer Solar system such as Titan and brought to Mars. Comets are another potential source of ammonia, as well as oxygen and hydrogen. Since ammonia is mostly nitrogen by weight, addition of a large volume of this material would nudge the atmosphere toward one similar in composition to Earth's. Once the atmosphere thickens, algae or genetically engineered plant life could be introduced to release and concentrate oxygen.

Other techniques to terraform Mars' atmosphere include detonating thermonuclear weapons on the surface to vaporize the crust and kick up dust and gases, bombarding the planet with hydrogen and helium harvested from gas giants like Jupiter, or adding chlorofluorocarbons to warm the atmosphere. One of the biggest issues with engineering Mars' atmosphere is keeping the gases within the atmosphere once introduced; oxygen tends to sequester into rock, limestone, rust, and sand. Oxygen can be harnessed from rocks by heating or electrolysis, but this requires an energy input and this expensive energy would be wasted if the oxygen wouldn't remain in the atmosphere. Likewise, hydrogen and helium tend to leave the atmosphere and drift into space because they're so light.

While Saturn's largest moon, Titan, is a candidate for terraforming in its own right, the high concentration of nitrogen and methane in its atmosphere are appealing raw materials to use for terraforming a planet like Mars. To recap, the raw materials exist within the Solar System to adjust whatever gases necessary to make an Earthlike atmosphere on many candidate planets or moons. For instance, Titan and Venus have extra nitrogen, Jupiter has extra hydrogen, and most planets have oxygen embedded in rock that could be extracted. With careful planning, scientists can determine the most economically and technologically viable option to pursue. The key hurdle will be the economic burden of pursuing any of the aforementioned atmosphere-altering projects.

Water

Early in its history Mars had liquid water on its surface, though all has since turned to ice. Enough trapped water may exist in Mars' polar ice caps to recreate about 1/7th of its former ocean. This furnishes us with the opportunity to nuke Mars' ice caps to release carbon dioxide, thicken the atmosphere and hopefully melt the ice into liquid water. Alternatively, satellite mirrors could be constructed to reflect the sun's rays onto the ice caps to melt them and provide a comparable result.

Transitioning away from Mars to generalize the subject for any candidate in our Solar System, comets are the top contender for acquisition of water in many cases. The idea is to redirect comets toward a planet or moon and blow them up right before impact, unleashing ice shards onto the body to create seas once the ice melts. While redirecting a comet may at first seem an insurmountable task, the European Space Agency's *Philae* lander has already made a successful landing onto a comet nucleus in 2014; the path to making a rendezvous with a comet has already been paved. What remains now is to develop the technology to manipulate the comet's orbit.

Temperature

For most candidate bodies, manipulating temperature isn't as difficult as manipulating the atmosphere or water levels. For hot planets like Mercury or Venus, satellite solar shades could be built to block out a portion of the sun's rays and cool the surface. Since Mercury's day lasts as long as 60 Earth days and Venus' lasts 243 Earth days, a more complex system of solar mirrors could be employed to redirect light to artificially recreate a day-night cycle that mimics Earth's. However, humans could still survive on these planets even if each day lasted several months; having artificial 24-hour days is more of a luxury than a necessity.

At the other end of the spectrum, for planets in orbits further away from the Sun than Earth's we could concentrate sunlight using satellite mirrors, somewhat akin to using a magnifying glass to concentrate sunlight onto a smaller area. Again, relative to the challenge of terraforming the atmosphere, altering temperature would typically be *relatively* a bit more trivial. Day lengths for the outer planets are typically shorter than those for inner planets. Fortunately, the length of Martian day is right near 24 hours so no fancy mirrors would be necessary to alter Mars' day. Jupiter, Saturn, Uranus and Neptune all have less than 24-hour days, so it may be worthwhile to artificially lengthen these days for future long-term settlements on these planets.

Summary

Whether moving gaseous material, steering a comet into a planet, or building a planet-sized sun shade, humanity must be able to more economically enter into and return from space. Traditional rocket travel is simply too expensive. Thus, cheap space travel, whether via mass driver, skyhook, or another of the dozens of envisioned megastructures, is a prerequisite to any terraforming project. Many of these technologies rely an electromagnetic acceleration rather than chemical propulsion and would be able to substantially drop the price of space travel. Any invention that effects an abated overall price tag will play a part in augmenting the economic viability and therefore the prospects of terraforming.

Alternatives to terraforming include bioforming and paraterraforming. **Bioforming** involves using genetic engineering techniques to increase humans' or other organisms' ability to survive on alien planets containing non Earth-like environments. At the intersection of terraforming and bioforming, scientists could genetically engineer bacteria to create organisms that flourish in conditions of another planet and to produce byproducts that alter the atmosphere to create an eventually habitable space for plants and animals. **Paraterraforming** involves creating an inhabitable microhabitat on a larger body, such as by building a closed dome to terraform just part of a planet, much like a greenhouse for plants on earth.

Though even the most basic terraforming projects can take centuries, such lengthy projects aren't without precedent. For instance, the Angkor Wat Temple in Cambodia, the ancient Mayan Chichen Itza, Stonehenge, and the Great Wall of China each took centuries to complete. Humans can be incredibly persistent at times. While you or I will almost assuredly never see a terraforming project completed, we could conceivably commence a project that could be completed by our descendants.

Space Topic 2: Launch Loop

Status of the technology: Mostly a thought experiment at this point. Design blueprints have been drafted and most aspects of the technology are surprisingly feasible.

What to expect: The risk, sheer scale, and cost of the project will likely dissuade investors and other stakeholders from moving forward in the short- to medium-term. Reusable rockets will likely increase in popularity as the most feasible option for cost-effective payload launch into space over the next few decades. As the science of building active structures (discussed below) progresses, we may discover increased interest in building a Launch Loop as a cheaper method to get payloads into orbit. We may reasonably expect to see construction on a Launch Loop by 2075.

Launching satellites or other objects into space via traditional chemical-propellant rockets currently costs several hundred dollars per kilogram, which renders many projects containing heavy payloads prohibitively expensive. Reducing the per-kilogram launch cost for payloads sent to space is vital to any of humanity's long-term aspirations in space, including asteroid mining, setting up space colonies, or terraforming other planets. For this reason, a variety of technologies have been proposed as alternatives to rocket-based launch. A few examples are the skyhook, slingatron, space fountain, mass driver, space gun, ram accelerator, pneumatic tower, rotovator, orbital ring, and blast wave accelerator, and this list is by no means exhaustive. The names of many of these proposals can give you a general idea of the underlying mechanisms they use to launch payloads into space. They exhibit a range of technical feasibilities but none will be ready for commercialization any time soon. Here we will discuss the Launch Loop, which is one of the more popular proposals for non-rocket space launch and is also one of the more theoretically feasible technologies.

The Launch Loop, also known as the Lofstrom Loop for its original designer Keith Lofstrom, is an elevated railway track that would launch magnetically levitating objects into orbit via electromagnetic acceleration. Though the technology seems farfetched, the plans for the structure including fine details of the components are lucidly explicated by Lofstrom. It would be placed above an ocean and would be about 2,000 kilometers long and 80 kilometers in altitude. It's designed with the intention of human travel; the 2,000 kilometer length of track would allow for a semi-comfortable 3g acceleration to reach orbital velocity, about 10,000 meters per second, by the end of the track. The track would need to be longer if certain payloads needed to be accelerated at a more comfortable pace. Likewise, the track could be shorter for non-human objects that can handle more than 3g's.

Eighty kilometers in altitude is a sweet spot. It's high enough to vastly decrease air resistance compared to sea level due to the thinning of the atmosphere, but it's low enough that most incoming meteors and space debris will be vaporized by the time they reach this level in the atmosphere. It's also too low for space trash to be in a stable orbit because enough air exists to decelerate a passive object and decay its speed enough for it to fall out of the sky.

At first thought, building such a structure may seem completely infeasible. How could we possibly build an 80 kilometer high railway when the tallest building in the world, the Burj Khalifa, is less than one single kilometer tall? The solution to building such a huge structure is **active support**. Most buildings today are passively supported static structures; the weight of the building is borne passively by the materials that comprise it, putting the structure in compression. Building tall structures in this manner puts huge compressive pressures on the materials at the bottom of the structure since this material must support the weight of everything above. Active support, in contrast, uses active power input to shape the structure and keep it in a stable configuration.

As an analogy for how the active support would work in a Launch Loop, imagine a powerful water hose. We could shoot water from the hose in an arc in the sky. For the purposes here, imagine that this is laminar flow and that all the water particles stay together rather than splitting up into chaotic spray. At the end of the arc, all of the water particles fall into a basin. Now imagine a second hose right by that basin, shooting water into a similar arc and landing in a basin by the first hose. We could theoretically sit an object like a plate on top of the arcs and it would remain in the air. It would spin because the two streams are moving in opposite directions, but the streams would actively support the plate. Now we can make a small alteration; if we envelop the streams in a very thin sheath or hose, they would maintain their same path but the plate would no longer spin.

Now instead of water imagine an iron cable moving at 30,000 miles per hour inside a frictionless sheath and you've got a Launch Loop. The visible part of the Launch Loop would be a continuous sheath and inside the sheath would be another continuous tube called the rotor. The iron rotor would be moving inside a vacuum in the tube of the sheath at blistering speeds but would be pushed away from the sides of the sheath via a magnetic field, rendering it frictionless. The rotor's speed would force it to take the shape of an arch, lifting the structure. The Launch Loop would have a station at the beginning and end of the 2,000 kilometer track, pinning the structure to the ground, providing power to the rotor, and looping the rotor around to begin its journey toward the opposite end. This creates a continuous loop, and the momentum of the rotary belt transfers the weight of the system to the ends.

Active support is a very different type of support than what most humans are familiar with. It's not compressive nor tensile. It's not unlike the active burning of rocket fuel that provides active support to keep a rocket in the air, countering gravity's pull. Since the structure supports itself with the kinetic energy of the moving rotor, it wouldn't be under extreme tensile or compressive pressures. Thus, the Launch Loop would not require exotic materials like the space elevator (discussed in a separate entry) would to achieve technological feasibility.

Since the Launch Loop would be a dynamic structure that would require an energy input to remain stable, operators would be able to control the shape as well as the height of the resulting structure. The railway could be lowered to float on the surface of the ocean to do repairs, maintenance or construction. Once the structure would be ready to be put back into service, the rotors would be started up, and the structure would lift off from the surface of the water and rise to 80 kilometers in altitude.

So, how feasible is the Launch Loop? The launch of the vehicle itself would follow most of the same principles as a maglev bullet train, which is already proven technology. The rotor that would provide structure to the loop would also power the vehicle and would necessarily need to be moving at orbital velocity. This is theoretically feasible but quite dangerous and power intensive. We currently have the technology for all the materials we would need to build the structure. Being so long and thin, weather issues are a real concern, as is the heating of the system. The massive power input and fast-moving parts would create a great deal of waste heat. Advances in the science of superconductors would largely ameliorate this issue. From a purely technological standpoint, there aren't any huge unanswered scientific or engineering questions that are hindering the realization of the concept.

Estimates of the cost of launching payload into space using a Launch Loop are as low as $3 per kilogram, though this may be inordinately optimistic. Even at $30 or $100 per kilogram, the Launch Loop would be an economic leap forward over traditional rocketry. At a high level, the Loop is essentially a giant conveyor belt that would have the capacity to make many launches per hour. It would take much less setup and preparation between launches than chemical rocket launches. It's entirely feasible that only a few years of operation would be necessary to recoup the estimated $10 billion price tag.

<u>Space Topic 3: Dyson sphere</u>

Status of the technology: Only a thought experiment at this point. Solar sailing and space construction technologies are nowhere near sophisticated enough to make serious plans to build a Dyson Sphere.

What to expect: Don't expect anything within your lifetime. Your grandchildren's grandchildren's grandchildren's lifetimes? Perhaps, we'll have to wait and see. Making an absolute estimation of when humanity may build a Dyson Sphere with present knowledge is an exercise in futility.

In the 1960's, theoretical physicist Freeman Dyson theorized that technologically advanced civilizations would experience progressive interminable increases in energy demand as their technology improves. Eventually a civilization's planet would no longer have sufficient energy to support the inhabitants, so they would instead seek energy from the star that their planet orbits. Humans, therefore, might also eventually demand a higher energy output than resources on Earth alone can provide, so we would look to harness more energy directly from our Sun. Dyson proposed a system of orbiting structures close to the sun that would harness a much greater percentage of the Sun's total energy output than the amount that currently reaches Earth.

Though the name "**Dyson Sphere**" insinuates a fixed structure, building a fixed structure around the Sun is not only impossible with current engineering technologies, but also onerous even with hypothetical futuristic technologies. Dyson instead imagined a series of objects orbiting the sun independently. A better descriptor is a **Dyson Swarm**, a collection of solar powered satellites that would produce power and distribute it to Earth via wireless energy transfer. This could be constructed incrementally and would be technologically possible within a reasonable period of time into the future. A Dyson Swarm would, in essence, provide humans with unlimited energy.   However, to procure enough materials to build such a swarm, humanity would likely have to disassemble most of an entire planet. Since Mercury is already close to the Sun and is rich in metals like iron and nickel, it would be the most likely candidate for the project.

A **Dyson Bubble** is a similar proposal to the Dyson Swarm, but it would employ **statites**, satellites suspended by the radiation pressure on huge light sails that would counteract the star's gravity. When the forces from the outward push of the radiation pressure from sunlight and the inward pull of the sun's gravity are equal, the statite would hover over the sun. Like the Dyson Swarm, this could also be constructed incrementally.   Advances in materials science would be necessary to develop the statites, as the weight per area would need to be about 100 times less dense than a sheet of paper or 4 times less dense than any current lightsail technology for the satellite to remain stationary at an orbit near the distance that Earth currently orbits.   As an aside, radiation pressure and light sailing are expounded in a separate article on solar sailing below.

A **Dyson Shell** is the hypothetical rigid sphere briefly mentioned earlier. It would completely envelop and capture 100% of the Sun's energy, which would be trillions of times the current power consumption of humans. The technological challenges of constructing such a structure are monumental. The shell would be vulnerable to impacts and it could conceivably accidentally drift directly into the sun. Since the shell would likely have to be as far from the Sun as Earth currently is for the materials to resist burning or melting, it's questionable whether enough materials even exist in the solar system to build it.

In the process of harnessing and using incoming starlight using a rigid shell, a civilization would produce waste heat which would be radiated out mostly in the infrared part of the electromagnetic spectrum. Thus, one method of looking for intelligent alien life is to search for a star that emits more infrared light then we would expect based on natural models alone. Upon discovery, we could look into an artificial origin as a possible explanation for the anomaly. Though humanity is nowhere near being able to build a Dyson Shell ourselves, Dyson's thought experiment has provided some direction to the search for extraterrestrial intelligence, as astronomers are actively scanning other galaxies for spikes in infrared radiation.

If you're optimistic about intelligent alien life, a star 1,470 light years away called KIC 8462852 exhibits unusual fluctuations and dimming of about 22% of the star's total luminosity. Since no natural phenomena perfectly fit the data, some astronomers have suggested the fluctuations could be an artifact from a Dyson Swarm. This hypothesis has since been mostly discredited by experts since certain wavelengths of light dim more than others, which is more consistent with dimming from dust or gas than dimming from an opaque object, which would dim all wavelengths equally. In all likelihood, it's probably a head-on asteroid belt, but we don't know for sure. Other suggestions of natural causes include a cloud of disintegrating comets, a debris field, dust, or the coalescing of a smaller star. Research continues, and the Search for Extraterrestrial Intelligence (SETI Institute) is actively monitoring the star.

Space Topic 4: Solar Sailing

Status of the technology: Proven concept. Several spacecraft using solar sails as the primary source of mobility have been successful.   Most recently, the Planetary Society's Lightsail 2 spacecraft was launched in the summer of 2019 to conduct experiments on using the sail to manipulate its orbit around Earth.

What to expect: Expect the technology to slowly replace traditional rocketry in specific scenarios such as long-distance or interstellar travel. Though faster and more efficient than chemical rocketry, solar sailing takes a long time to build up speed and cannot make quick or agile adjustments to its flight path. Thus, it will likely be relegated to a specific niche, at least for the foreseeable future.

Anybody who's shot a shotgun has felt Newton's third law of motion in action. Propelling the pellets forward results in an equal and opposite force in the opposite direction, the "kick" of the gun. Traditional rockets and spacecraft operate on this same principle. They're propelled by rocket fuel that exits one end of the rocket at high speed which pushes the rocket in the opposite direction. The problem here is that the amount of rocket fuel a rocket can carry is finite. Eventually the fuel will run out. What if this didn't have to be the case?

A new technology called **solar sailing** will allow spacecraft to travel the cosmos without ever running out of fuel. Solar sailing is analogous to windsailing, but the propulsive force is sunlight rather than wind. A solar sailing spacecraft would have a sail that reflects sunlight, and the reflected light imparts a radiation pressure that pushes on the sail. Again analogous to wind sailing, solar sailing spacecraft would be able to either travel away from the sun or tack inwards toward the sun much like a sailboat can tack into the wind.

The radiation pressure force is too weak to be observed on Earth except under controlled experiments with fine-tuned measuring instruments. However, in outer space it's usually the second largest force acting on objects after gravity. The force it imparts in outer space is small at any single instant, but it can have a large net effect over an extended period of time. The technology is also very scalable. Right now, all the test missions run so far only have sails with square footage the size of a small apartment. However, we could theoretically scale it up to a football field or larger. It's one of the few technologies with a high enough upper bound on speed that could allow humans to exit our own solar system and visit other star systems.

The effect of radiation pressure is incorporated into the mathematical models that engineers use to calculate all flight paths to Mars and other planets. If they ignored the effect of the pressure from sunlight the spacecrafts would miss their marks by thousands of miles. Using solar sailing as a primary rather than supplementary means of propulsion has been successfully achieved. In 2010, the Japanese launched the IKAROS spacecraft, which was the first spacecraft to use a solar sail as its main propulsion mechanism and the first to succeed in using the technology. It completed its planned mission to Venus and is now orbiting the sun.

The Planetary Society, a non-profit organization currently led by Bill Nye, crowdfunded and created the LightSail spacecraft that's about the size of a loaf of bread that deployed a 32 square meter (345 square feet) sail once it reached space. The sail is made of mylar, the thin metallic silvery polyester film used in space blankets. They completed a test flight in low Earth orbit with the Lightsail in 2015 and launched their second solar sailing spacecraft in July 2019 to use the sail to provide power to raise its orbit around Earth.

The benefits of solar sailing over traditional rockets are obvious:

1) Lower cost of operations
2) Fewer moving parts
3) Longer operating lifetimes
4) No running out of fuel

However it does have drawbacks:

1) The sail must be huge compared to the size of the satellite, making the technology impractical for very heavy satellites
2) It takes time for cumulative photons to hit the sail and contribute speed. Thus the technology is more useful for long-distance missions

Various methods have been proposed to take the general principle behind radiation pressure-driven propulsion to the extreme. They go by many exotic names such as beam powered propulsion, directed energy propulsion, laser sailing, and photonic laser thrusting. The idea behind all of these ideas is to provide the sails with active directed radiation that's more concentrated than sunlight, usually by shooting lasers at the sails.

Traditional chemical accelerants cannot reach speeds sufficient for interstellar travel, but these laser-powered technologies may open up other star systems for exploration. With the concentrated beam of photons from photonic propulsion or laser thruster sails it's mathematically feasible to get to Mars in as little as 3 days or to reach speeds of up to several percent of the speed of light, several hundred times faster than any spaceships we've built so far.

The technology will continue to be developed, as the Japanese are planning to launch IKAROS's successor, OKEANOS, in the late 2020's to be sent to Jupiter and the Trojan Asteroids near Jupiter. IKAROS had a 14 x 14 meter sail, and OKEANOS will have a much larger 40 x 40 meter sail. Several similar projects are proposed to launch in the next 15 years to test the feasibility of various maneuvers using solar sails.

<u>Space Topic 5: Asteroid mining</u>

Status of the technology: Little is stopping us technologically, as we have the ability to launch craft into space and land on asteroids. For instance, the Japanese Hayabusa2 is currently taking exploratory samples of an asteroid and should return them to Earth in December 2020. We currently have no methods to mine minerals in zero gravity but that's only a minor hurdle compared to the challenge of the launch and rendezvous.

What to expect: Money is the biggest factor hindering us from launching a full-scale asteroid mining project. However, the economics look better every day. Mineral deposits are becoming rarer on Earth, whereas the price of space travel is dropping. Several companies claim they'll be mining by 2030 or 2035, but I feel that those dates are a tad optimistic and may be rooted in generating media hype or securing venture capital investment. I hope I'll be proven wrong, but I wouldn't hold my breath waiting for a true initial asteroid mining mission to be launched before 2040.

Asteroid mining may seem like a figment of science fiction, but companies like Planetary Resources and Deep Space Industries are actively pursuing the venture right now. Humanity may even be less than a decade away from active mining and this isn't just a vanity project. With the exploding global population and high demand for elements that are rare in Earth's crust, elements such as gold, silver, copper, phosphorus and zinc may be depleted in the next 50 years. Many of these elements are vital components of electronics that will bear an ever-increasing demand. Thus, the economics of asteroid mining will become more practical every year as technology increases and global deposits of rare earth metals and other rare elements decrease.

Four billion years ago, as the early molten Earth cooled, most of the valuable heavy elements sank to the core and are thus rare on Earth's surface. In contrast, asteroids don't have a core and their surfaces are often replete with rare elements. Though mundane at first glance, asteroids are far from simply low-value rocks. Mining these could surfeit humanity's appetite for most metals rare in Earth's crust.

The elemental composition varies from asteroid to asteroid but many contain a suite of commercially attractive elements. Some asteroids contain organic material and water, whereas others are high in valuable platinum, indium, rhodium, silver and gold, and still others are high in lower-value metals like iron, copper, lead and nickel. Some of the rarest elements on Earth like osmium, iridium, platinum, and palladium are present on asteroids at 100 times higher concentrations than on Earth.

Asteroids that are high in water, carbon, and phosphorus are not profitable on their own but could serve as support and refueling stations for mining activities on other asteroids. The water could be extracted to produce drinking water and air to support human life, as well as split into hydrogen and oxygen for use as fuel. One water-rich asteroid could contain enough fuel for every rocket that's been launched so far in history. Currently it costs around $20,000 to send a liter of water into deep space, so the economic incentive to produce water in space is clear.

Many classes of minerals have hydrogen and oxygen embedded within their chemical structure, even minerals that don't feel wet like talc (baby powder) or slate (chalkboards). Once an asteroid with enough water embedded in its chemical composition is found, sections could be heated to extract the water. Setting up a refueling station on an asteroid that operates on this principle would drastically reduce the cost of space travel compared to transporting the fuel from Earth.

The holy grail for prospective asteroid miners is the mining of platinum-group metals, which are in high demand on Earth for everything from catalysts in oil refineries to electronics to jewelry.

A single asteroid rich in platinum-group metals could contain more of these metals than all of what's been mined in all of human history. Such high-value metals would predictably be transported back to Earth for sale.   In contrast, low-value metals like iron, cobalt and nickel wouldn't be profitable to bring back to Earth so they could be used for construction of asteroid colonies or space colonies.

So, how does mining actually occur? Similar to the gold rush of the mid-1800's where the first arrivals in California could find large gold nuggets just lying around on the ground in shallow streams, the initial mining of asteroids could be as easy as raking up loose materials that lay on the surface. Machines could scrape the surface to remove any loose material or use a magnetic rake to pick up any magnetic metals. Later, drilling, harpooning or other methods would become necessary. If the geology of the rock is well-characterized, a shaft could be dug to extract materials located below the surface.

Three primary methods exist to achieve the end goal of bringing processed asteroid material to market on Earth:

1) Extract raw materials from the asteroid and return them to Earth for processing. This is the most straight-forward method and will likely be the first method of asteroid mining attempted.

2) Process the materials on site at the asteroid and return processed materials to Earth. The main benefit of this method is the lower transport cost back to Earth since the material will be value-added and more profitable per unit of weight when transported back to Earth. Transportation of materials in space is still very expensive so there's a tangible benefit to shedding every kilogram possible before transporting materials back to Earth.

3) Nudge the asteroid into a safe orbit around the moon, Earth, or to the International Space Station for processing. This

method has obvious and enormous risks and will likely only be tested after both other methods find success.

Altogether, the net worth of the materials that make up asteroids are in the quintillions of dollars. If an asteroid mining entrepreneur can successfully start up operations, it's quite possible that he or she will become the world's first trillionaire. Due to the high capital requirement, this venture would likely aggrandize somebody who was already a billionaire or successful and influential entrepreneur before undertaking the project. Powerful people like Peter Diamandis (serial space and biotech entrepreneur), Eric Schmidt (Google executive chairman), James Cameron (wealthy and influential filmmaker and philanthropist), and Larry Page (Google cofounder) already have a stake in the industry.

So what's the holdup? The truth is that space travel is still expensive and cost is a huge hurdle. Now that space travel is becoming privatized companies are bringing down the price, but successfully launching a mining mission would still take hundreds of millions of dollars. A great deal of testing would be required because with this amount of money on the line it's imperative that the first real mission be launched with success in mind.

Another challenge is communication. It would take several minutes to communicate from Earth back-and-forth to the landers on the asteroid. This wouldn't be an efficient way to mine, so the alternative is automation. Of course automation introduces an entire new suite of technical challenges of its own. Humans have succeeded in its Mars missions even with the communications delay but these were publicly funded research experiments. Time and efficiency weren't as important as a commercial project.

Yet another challenge is the mining technique. No techniques to mine in zero gravity currently exist so these would inevitably have to be developed. Various ideas are being tested, such as physical digging with harpoons or optical mining, which would dig holes into asteroids by concentrating sunlight onto a small area.

<u>Space Topic 6: Space elevator</u>

Status of the technology: We currently have no material light and strong enough to construct the tether. Advances in materials technology are a necessity for this concept to move forward. Besides the tether, most other aspects of the technology are surprisingly feasible.

What to expect: There's a great economic incentive to actually construct the elevator.   Governments and billionaires have expressed a desire to fund the project if scientists and engineers can overcome the technological challenges.   Realistically the earliest we could expect an elevator would be around 2080.

The idea for a space elevator was first introduced in 1979 in a Sci-Fi novel called the Fountain of Paradise. The structure would be just what it sounds like: an elevator that could take you from ground level to space. The general idea is technologically possible on paper, but economic and materials science hurdles would need to be overcome before we could begin construction on one.

Plans for space elevators differ in the details, but most have four basic components: base, tether, counterweight, and climber. The base would be anchored to Earth and serve as the anchor point for the tether and the loading zone for the climber. The tether would be an extremely light and strong cable that would reach from the base on Earth's surface into space. The counterweight would be attached to the end of the tether in space. It needs to be huge; many plans call for wrangling an asteroid and bringing it into Earth's orbit to use as the counterweight. Lastly, the climber would be somewhat similar to an elevator car we're familiar with. It would climb up and down the tether.

The competing forces of gravity at the bottom of the tether and centrifugal force on the counterweight tied to the top of the tether due to the rotation of the Earth would result in the tether being taut and in tension. The goal is to achieve geostationary orbit, which means that the speed and orbital height of the system directly matches the rotation of the Earth, and the cable would remain directly over the base on Earth. Geostationary orbit is around 35,786 kilometers above Earth, which is the magic number where the gravity pulling downwards and the centrifugal force pulling upwards will need to be in equilibrium. To achieve this equilibrium, the counterweight would likely need to be about 36,000 to 100,000 kilometers above Earth's surface, which is about 3 to 8 times the diameter of Earth. At the upper end of the range, the counterweight would be more than a quarter of the distance to the moon.

An analogy can help elucidate how the space elevator would work. Imagine holding the string of a Yo-Yo and spinning the toy quickly around and around in a circular motion. Your hand will provide the energy for the Yo-yo to make its circular motion. Now imagine a beetle on your finger. If the insect climbs off of your finger and walks down the rope towards the Yo-yo, it will eventually gain more and more rotational speed as it travels distally. The beetle only needs to do minimal work to gain a lot of speed. Your hand is doing most of the work.

A space elevator can be visualized in the same way. The rotation of the Earth provides the energy. A space elevator will extend up to 100,000 kilometers above a base point on Earth, and a counterweight at 100,000 kilometers acts similarly to the weighted Yo-Yo, whose weight creates centrifugal force that provides tension. The counterweight both holds the tether up and brings the center of balance of the system into space. Much like the beetle only needing to walk down the string, in a space elevator the only active energy input necessary is for the climber to crawl up the tether towards the counterweight. The rotation of the Earth gives the climber the sideways movement without artificially needing to expend energy to create the lateral movement.

An object being in orbit means that it is falling towards the Earth but moving fast enough laterally that the curvature of the Earth keeps the object from ever getting closer to Earth's surface. Said another way, the object is moving sideways faster than gravity pulls it down, so that the curvature of the planet slopes away as fast as the object falls down toward it. A rocket must propel itself both upwards and very quickly sideways to reach a stable orbit. In contrast and as aforementioned, the only energy requirement for a space elevator is the upwards movement, which greatly reduces the energy necessary to achieve orbit. This energy savings is at the heart of the economic incentive to build a space elevator. At present, it costs about $5,000 to get a single kilogram to space using traditional rockets. However, a space elevator could theoretically get a kilogram into orbit to as low as $200 per kilogram. Since getting large satellites into space currently costs millions to billions of dollars in transportation costs alone, the tens of billions of dollars for the price tag of a space elevator could be recouped after launching only a few giant satellites. The climber could climb up the tether to carry a satellite to space, release it into orbit, then climb back down to pick up another.

Various competitions have been held since the 2000's to inspire technologies relevant to space elevators. Early competitions were general and included prizes for climber technology, but more recent competitions have all focused on the biggest glaring problem hindering the elevator: the tether. We currently have the materials we need to build the anchor, elevator car and counterweight, but it will take large advances in materials science to find a material light enough and strong enough to serve as the tether. In addition to low weight and high strength, it also needs to be flexible, affordable, stable, corrosion resistant, radiation resistant, and able to withstand impacts from orbital debris. Thus, recent competitions have almost exclusively focused on materials technology, with top prospects for the tether being exotic materials like graphene, carbon nanotubes, diamond nanothreads, and boron nitride nanotubes.

Modern ideas for the base are typically huge mobile seafaring platforms. Alternatively, it could be built at the top of a mountain, reducing the total tether size needed and reducing some of the pull of gravity, which is higher near earth's core.

The counterweight could serve as a space station or launching point for space missions. Ideas for the counterweight include a satellite, asteroid, or simply extending the tether a few hundred thousand extra kilometers out into space until it imparts the same centrifugal force that a heavy counterweight would have.

Powering the climber would still need to be worked out. Since solar power is too weak to provide sufficient power, nuclear power and laser propulsion systems have been proposed. However, figuring this out is only a minor detail in comparison to the monumental challenge of building the tether.

Though building a space elevator would be the single largest construction project humanity has ever tackled, it may make economic sense. That being said, even "simple" facets of the project are still under debate. For one, there isn't yet a consensus on whether we should start the tether at the base and launch it into space or start in space and lower the tether down to earth. It's critical that the project be done right the first time. In the event of a catastrophe such as the tether breaking near the ground the counterweight and tether would be sent off into space. If the tether breaks near the counterweight, the tether will fall onto Earth. In either scenario, billions of dollars would be lost. Since the stakes are so high, it may be more practical to first develop a space elevator on the Moon. Since the Moon has weaker gravity than the Earth, currently available materials like Kevlar would be strong and light enough to build the tether there. Plus, construction challenges could be addressed in a smaller-scale environment.

Sector 3: Sustenance

<u>Sustenance Topic 1: Vertical Farming</u>

Status of the technology: The technology is proven, as hundreds of vertical farms are in operation all over the world. Active farms reside in many urban centers like Singapore, Vancouver, and in various cities in the United States and United Kingdom. Lack of economic viability is bankrupting many startups in the medium term; once investment money runs out most companies go belly-up. About one-quarter have managed to become profitable, so there is hope for the industry.

What to expect: Improvements in electrical efficiency and the discovery and maturation of best practices are necessary for long-term success and profitability of the industry. Most present-day companies grow almost exclusively leafy greens since these products require little light and have high margins. We can expect to see vertically-farmed greens on shelves in the next 5 years, but it'll be several more years until fruits and grains become profitable, if at all. Since leafy greens make up only a small fraction of the total produce market, the impact that vertical farming will have on agriculture depends upon whether other crops can be profitable grown in this manner.

With the exploding global population, humanity is headed for a crisis. In the next few decades, the agricultural industry in many areas may simply not produce enough food to meet demand. There are also ethical and environmental discussions to be had regarding deforestation and pesticide runoff into waterways, but that's beyond the scope here. Long story short, traditional agriculture will not suffice if the world's population continues increasing to 10 billion and beyond. Various methods to meet these exigencies such as reducing food waste or improving yields may incrementally ameliorate the issue, but it will take a paradigm-shifting technology like carniculture (another topic discussed in this book) or vertical farming to address the problem in the long term.

Vertical farms are indoor areas that grow stacked layers of plants, usually 7 to 15 layers high. Most environmental variables such as lighting, water levels, temperature and humidity are artificially controlled. By nature of being indoors and shielded from the environment, the plants experience no seasonality, so crops can be grown year-round.

Some vertical farms use soil but most use more sophisticated technologies like aeroponics, hydroponics, or aquaponics. All three of these use less water than soil farming. In hydroponics, the soil is replaced with a water and nutrient mix. In aeroponics, the plants are grown on a membrane or cloth, with the roots being misted with a nutrient and water solution. Aquaponics is a more complex version of hydroponics where the plants are grown in an aquatic ecosystem alongside other organisms like fish and aquatic bacteria. Nutrients are cycled back and forth between the aquatic creatures in the delicate and balanced aquaponic system.

Most promising vertical farming companies utilize the aeroponic approach. Macronutrients and micronutrients are dissolved into the water that is sprayed directly onto the roots, so the plants don't need to build elaborate root systems to fight for nutrients. As a result, the plants focus more growth upwards into the shoots and leaves, and growth cycles can be reduced by as much as 50% over traditional soil farming. An added benefit is that no pesticides are used and consumers aren't obligated to wash the produce before consumption.

Large vertical farming operations, often termed plant factories, are usually treated similar to clean rooms like those used in drug manufacturing. This ensures that the plants are shielded from insects and disease without using pesticides. The indoor nature of the operations also protects the company from losses due to birds, droughts and most natural disasters. Plant factory operations are usually built in large abandoned buildings, such as warehouses or retired factories and manufacturing sites. The buildings are retrofitted to allow the indoor environment to be carefully controlled. The atmosphere in the farms is often enriched with carbon dioxide to further improve productivity.

The benefits to farming vertically include:

1) Reduced travel distance for the food to reach consumers, also known as "food miles"
2) Increased availability of fresh produce to urban areas and city centers
3) Water savings. Some farms that collect rainwater or recycle transpired or evaporated water use as little as 0.5% to 5% of the water traditional farms use
4) Less need for land. Farmland can be returned to forests and other biomes
5) No need for pesticides and herbicides
6) Decreased requirement for travel and efficient logistics allows plants to be picked when ripe, rather than before they become ripe
7) Yield per square meter up to 100 times that of traditional farms
8) The climate-controlled and carbon dioxide doped environment can cut cycle times down to around 50%
9) No seasonality. Crops can grow year round

Today's plant factories target premium range products out of necessity. It is unclear whether they will be able to compete on price with traditional farms for the entire market rather than just the premium end of the market. Though premium or leafy green products represent only a small portion of the total market, vertical farms are poised to corner and dominate this market. However, to make a material ecological impact vertical farms will need to grow a wider range of produce, including high-volume commodity crops with thin margins. At present, grain agriculture takes up many times more land and water than the agriculture of greens.

To reduce costs, some farms shine pink, purple, or a combination of red and blue LED lights on their plants. Sunlight includes all of the colors of the visible electromagnetic spectrum, but plants do not utilize all frequencies of light. Plants typically only use the red and blue portion of the electromagnetic spectrum, so emitting only these light frequencies that plants actually use can reduce electricity requirements. Since electricity is the largest cost for vertical farms and has largely contributed to the bankruptcy of many failed vertical farms, advancements in LED technology would directly aid vertical farming companies. It is unclear whether using artificial light will be sustainable for growing a wider range of crops in the near future. Some companies have built transparent vertical greenhouses to partially use sunlight as a light source, but the tradeoff is that farmers lose their ability to control lighting conditions. Powering the farms with renewable technologies like solar power may alleviate this issue and permit profitability.

The benefits of vertical farming are clear, but critics point to the energy inputs from artificial lighting and heating as potentially outweighing the benefits of growing food close to the consumer. If the power to operate the farm comes from the grid powered by fossil fuels, it may even result in a heavier negative environmental impact than a traditional farm. Either way, the vertical farming industry is poised for a boom, as continual improvements in renewable energy and LED technology will permit these farms to incrementally adopt technologies that will allow them to be both more environmentally friendly and more profitable.

<u>Sustenance Topic 2: Carniculture</u>

Status of the technology: Proof of concept complete. Unstructured meats like chicken nuggets or hamburgers are simple to make but striated or structured meat is still a few years away.

What to expect: Price is dropping substantially and is approaching that of traditional slaughtered-animal meat. Expect commercial lab-grown meats at small scale immediately. Scaling is proving difficult, so it might be around 2025 to 2030 before products becomes common in stores.

The human population is rapidly increasing, and feeding all of those people will be a great challenge for humanity moving forward. Livestock production requires a lot of land, and much of the deforestation currently occurring is being done to make room for livestock grazing and soybean farms to feed livestock. Continuing the current trajectory of agricultural production versus population growth, at some point in the late 21st century we'd likely begin realizing food shortages that would effect billions. A few solutions have been proposed, such as forcing all of humanity to become vegetarian to avoid the inefficient land-use of livestock production. A less authoritarian solution would allow people to continue to eat meat but would still address the ecosystem-destroying effects of livestock production. It goes by many names, including cultured meat, carniculture, clean meat, lab-grown meat, and slaughter-free meat, to name a few.

Lab-grown meat is exactly what it sounds like. Fortunately, much research on tissue regeneration in the healthcare industry is directly or indirectly translatable to growing meat for consumption. Advances in techniques to prepare skin grafts, grow transplant organs, or engineer tissue to treat muscular dystrophy have all provided valuable knowledge on how to grow biological tissue without an animal.

As a brief history, the first lab-grown meat was consumed in 2003, when some French scientists ate a small batch of lab-grown frog tissue. Things really picked up in 2013, when a Dutch professor produced the first hamburger produced solely from artificially grown cells, and it was eaten at a news conference with a famous food scientist and chef in attendance. The hamburger had a price tag of over $250,000 and took 2 years to produce. This publicity led to several startups being founded, and there has been much more research in the field since. In addition to the private startups, tens of academic research laboratories around the world are working on developing cultured meat.

To discuss how the process works, a quick refresher on stem cells is in order. Stem cells multiply very quickly and have **pluripotency**, which means that they can differentiate into many different tissues (muscle, bone, fat, etc). As stem cells progress toward their final tissue-type, they reproduce less quickly and lose their ability to differentiate into other tissue types. Different research teams have utilized any of the following as starter cells that are taken from a living animal:

1) Adult or embryonic stem cells, which reproduce extremely fast but must later be re-programmed into muscle tissue
2) Skeletal stem cells (known as myoblasts). These are precursors to muscle cells and are not as flexible as stem cells. They're typically located within muscle and repair muscle after injury.
3) Fully developed muscle cells, which grow very slowly but don't have to be reprogrammed.

Thus, we see a trade-off between speed of growth and difficulty in programming the cells into muscle. Some research teams prefer growing stem cells very rapidly and then later converting them to muscle. Other teams prefer the much simpler but time-consuming approach of directly growing fully-developed adult muscle cells. Still other teams take the middle-of-the-road approach and use *skeletal* stem cells, which don't multiply as fast as other stem cells but are still faster than adult muscle cells. To recap, undifferentiated stem cells proceed through the following path to become meat; at each stage, the proliferation decreases, but the types of cells they can produce also decreases:

Stem cells → myoblasts (muscle stem cells) → fully developed muscle cells

The starter cells are placed in a bioreactor that supplies the cells with all the nutrients necessary to grow and multiply. The cells need to be kept warm and have available all the oxygen, salts, sugars, and proteins that they would have access to when within the animal. The goal is to trick the cells into thinking they're still inside the animal. Typically the serum used to culture the cells is made from animal blood, which has ethical implications if the technology is to fully eliminate animal suffering. Some companies are using artificial intelligence algorithms to scan plant-based ingredients to find suitable compounds to eventually replace blood serum. Initial progress suggests that animal-based serums may be unnecessary within only a few years.

If the starter cells were stem cells, they would necessarily be given signaling proteins to prompt them to differentiate into muscle and fat cells once the stem cells grew to sufficient numbers. The meat needs to be grown on a scaffold to direct the structure. Stretching of the scaffold can simulate regular muscle movement which assists growth. Various scaffolds have been developed, and some can be edible. Inedible scaffolds must be removed before the final product is ready.

The technology and science of actually growing the cells is advanced enough for commercialization. However, scale and cost are the main hurdles for widescale implementation. It's now relatively easy to grow a few hamburgers, but growing literal tons of hamburger meat to supply grocery stores is an entirely different challenge. Luckily the price is dropping: The price for one pound of cultured beef was over a million dollars in 2008. This dropped to tens of thousands of dollars around 2015, and is now down to around $2,000 per pound or less. Though still expensive, it's likely that the price will continue to drop until a pound of cultured meat approximates the price of a pound of traditional meat within the next few years.

A secondary challenge is structuring the meat. It's relatively straightforward to make a chicken nugget or hamburger but making a chicken breast or steak is much harder. Scientists must interweave muscle and fat into a striated pattern, and making muscle tissue grow and cooperate in such a way is proving to be a daunting task. "Ground meat" products will be on the market several years before structured meat makes its first debut.

Overall, this technology has the propensity to revolutionize the food supply chain. We can harvest a few cells from an umbilical cord, muscle, or even a feather, and have a meal prepared in as little as 8 weeks. You could one day be eating an animal that's still running around alive. Lab-grown meat uses less land, water and energy, and the chance for disease is reduced to nearly zero. There are also safety benefits. For instance, tuna could be prepared with no mercury, and we also have the control to engineer the protein-to-fat content as well as the concentration of omega-3 and omega-6 fatty acids and other minerals in the final products.

Predictably, this technology is receiving pushback from vested agricultural interests. Egg boards, cattle ranchers, and other meat interests have all been on the attack, criticizing the technology or launching petitions to re-define meat to legally differentiate "real" meat from cultured meat. Regulation and law regarding the cultured meat industry is in its infancy, but in many countries jurisdiction will become a joint effort by food, agricultural and drug governing bodies. For instance, in the United States the United States Department of Agriculture (USDA) and the Food and Drug

Administration (FDA) have agreed to share oversight of lab-grown meat products.

Expect cultured meat products to hit the shelves in the near future, as several companies plan to commercialize lab-grown meat products within the next five years. One benefit of lab-grown meat is that traditionally expensive meats can be just as simple to produce as traditionally lower grade meats. A company called Just Foods is sourcing Wagyu Beef cells from Japan to market a lab-grown version of the world-renowned beef. Another benefit of cultured meat lies in the fact that it's possible to combine meats into new products. We could grow lobster and filet mignon cells together for a whole new type of surf-n-turf.

Though testing of the effects of consuming cultured meats have suggested that the practice is as safe as eating traditional meat, much of the population would necessarily need to become inured to eating the meat. Though some people are receptive of the idea, others express disgust at the practice. Either way, the technology is greying moral and ethical waters that used to be black and white since it will uncouple meat eating and animal suffering. People for the Ethical Treatment of Animals (PETA) seems to be fully on board with the technology. They keep up with the industry and regularly write articles like "A Cruelty-Free Future" and "A Chicken Tender that's Tender to Chickens". That's some good news for the vegans and vegetarians out there getting bored with insipid veggie burgers.

Sector 4: Science Fiction Technologies

SciFi Topic 1: Electromagnetic Pulse

Status of the technology: Various small-scale prototype electromagnetic pulse (EMP) weapons have been built and tested, especially for research into defense against EMP. We have the technology to build Sci-Fi-esque high-altitude nuclear EMPs that could take out electronics across an entire country. Simulations have been run to determine the effects of such a blast.

What to expect: The technology is available to launch very large EMP's that could disrupt electronics for thousands of square miles. Hopefully we can expect that countries will eschew use.

An electromagnetic pulse is an ephemeral burst of electromagnetic energy. The pulse is comprised of a combination of an electric field, magnetic field, electromagnetic radiation, and/or an electric current, but is often dominated by one form, depending on the source of the pulse. Though pulses are typically broad-band (multitude of frequencies), they contain frequencies lower than that of visible light, so they're invisible to the naked eye. Sources can be either natural or artificial.

Natural sources of EMPs include lightning, solar flares, meteors impacting earth or burning in the atmosphere, or coronal mass ejections from the Sun, which are quick releases of magnetized plasma from the outer layer of the Sun. A large coronal mass ejection called the Carrington event occurred in 1859, which caused bright colorful lights in the atmosphere that effectively turned night into day, started fires and took down telegraph systems over much of the world. A similar event in today's time would be catastrophic since we rely much more heavily on electronics. Smaller solar storms seem to occur around every 40 years or so which result in localized power outages, but in 2012 a huge storm similar in size to the Carrington event narrowly missed earth. It's not inconceivable that a freak coronal mass injection could take out electronics across large sections of the globe in the future.

There are many ways to create man-made EMP's even with simple supplies from your local hardware store, so for our purposes here we'll just discuss the heavy hitters that could create large EMPs. These large sources include power line surges and deliberately designed weapons. On the weapons front, these include non-nuclear sources and nuclear sources. Non-nuclear EMP weapons are smaller than nuclear sources but can be used more tactically to specifically disable certain targets. Non-nuclear sources operate by various means such as by releasing capacitor energy into antennae, using a microwave generator, and using a flux compression generator.

A nuclear EMP is the electric shockwave triggered by a nuclear blast. The destruction greatly increases if the warhead is detonated around 30 to 500 kilometers into the atmosphere, in which case the weapon is termed a high-altitude nuclear EMP. At 100 kilometers or more, the line of sight of the burst would cover the entire continental United States. However, it's not just the line of sight that makes a high-altitude nuclear EMP more destructive than one detonated at ground level. When detonated high in the atmosphere, the released gamma rays interact with and ionize particles like nitrogen and oxygen, knocking off their electrons. This creates an electric current in the mid-stratosphere that amplifies the EMP effect compared to a bomb detonated on the surface. The electric current interacts with the earth's magnetic field to produce microwaves. Upon reaching electrically sensitive objects, the fields couple with the object to produce damaging high current and voltage surges. A high-altitude warhead could theoretically fry electronics for hundreds of square miles.

It's difficult to quantify exactly how much damage a nuclear EMP would do. As a rule of thumb, electronics that are running at the time of the EMP would be more vulnerable than inactive equipment. High currents and voltages would be induced within electronic equipment which would temporarily disrupt or permanently damage equipment. Higher voltages would interfere with magnetic storage computer hard drives and destroy data. At low voltages such as around the periphery of the affected area, the effects would likely be limited to electrical noise that effects equipment, such as the screen freezing on a TV or a computer locking up. Though electronics would be destroyed and modern life would be brought to a halt, people would barely feel the blast.

<u>SciFi Topic 2: Cloaking Device</u>

Status of the technology: Still in the research phase. Laboratory prototypes have been developed. Initial cloaking success has been achieved in the microwave area of the electromagnetic spectrum.

What to expect: Improvements to metamaterial fabrication will be a necessity to successfully cloak objects in the visible light range of the electromagnetic spectrum. We might expect rudimentary cloaking devices in the visible range in the laboratory setting in the 2030s, and cloaking of larger objects or potential practical applications in the 2040s to 2050s.

Cloaking is the act of making an object invisible to the part of the electromagnetic spectrum with which the observer is viewing. From short wavelength to long wavelength, the electromagnetic spectrum is comprised of:

gamma rays → x-rays → ultraviolet → visible light → infrared → microwaves → radio waves

An object can be effectively cloaked if the object is invisible to whatever wavelength the observer is detecting. For human vision, an object can be cloaked if it's invisible in the visible light range, but it could still show up on radar (radio frequency), infrared detector, or other type of detector outside of the visible range.

For the purposes here, we'll focus on techniques and research toward cloaking as seen in Sci-Fi movies, which must be agnostic to the angle and position of the observer. As such, we'll eschew discussing in detail the Rochester Cloak, which has gotten media attention and *technically* cloaks an object but in reality is just a fancy mirror game. The clever mirror positioning does indeed seem to cloak the object, but proper functioning is fully dependent on the position of the observer. At a high level, four mirrors simply bend light around the object and rejoin the light behind the object, resulting in the light bypassing the object.

Achieving cloaking is much more challenging than stealth technology. To achieve stealth, the object must reflect electromagnetic radiation *away* from the detector so that no radiation bounces off of the object to enter the detector. Cloaking technology requires that the light is bent *around* the object to continue on its original trajectory. Incoming radiation can't be simply reflected away from the observer. The goal is to effectively create a black box in which no radiation enters the cloak and none leaves. Any incoming light, from any angle, must be steered around. This return of light to the original trajectory suppresses the shadow and creates the scenery behind the object.

Original research into cloaking occurred in the 1950s, which focused on surrounding items with plasma that absorbs incoming radiation. This doesn't make the object invisible to eyes, but it does make them invisible to radar. This initial research has contributed to the rise of stealth technology and laid the groundwork for more sophisticated cloaking technology.

A more modern type of cloaking called **optical camouflage** occurs when, from an observer's perspective, an object projects the background behind itself onto the foreground. This is the type of camouflage that cuttlefish, octopi and chameleons use. These animals attempt to fool the observer by projecting the colors of the background onto the side of the animal's body facing the observer. Artificial optical camouflage would be a man-made mimic of this natural technology. This technology is in fact technically feasible right now, but prototypes struggle with lag and distortion when the object moves. The technology works well only if the observer and target both remain still.

The most promising method to achieve full, passive, 360-degree cloaking is through the use of optical metamaterials. **Metamaterials** are artificial materials that exhibit exotic properties not seen in nature due to their nanoscale structure rather than composition. They're manufactured with repeating patterns that can interact with, bend, reflect, absorb, or otherwise manipulate electromagnetic waves. If properly constructed, these materials can steer electromagnetic waves around an object and then return them to their original trajectory rather than refracting or reflecting them, effectively rendering the object invisible.

All rays of electromagnetic radiation follow the same physical laws as light, regardless of their frequency. Thus, some current research is being conducted with microwaves, which are waves just outside and longer than visible light. In this way, it's easier to create experiments but demonstrated success should theoretically be scalable down to visible light. As an example, cloaking a 3-decimeter long cylinder from microwaves is analogous to cloaking a 1 micrometer long object from visible waves. It's much easier to manipulate the size and shape of an object that's the size of a can of vegetables or liter of soda than one that's smaller than the diameter of a human hair.

The theory behind cloaking with metamaterials is to use the materials to cancel scattering signatures of the naked object with the use of a metamaterial cloak. This is achieved using **negative index of refraction metamaterials** which can bend light in the opposite direction of its angle of incidence. This effectively cancels scattered waves by scattering positive light from the object and negative light from the metamaterial. Properly set up, this apparatus should provide invisibility for all angles of observation and all positions of the observer. As aforementioned, this is primarily being tested using microwaves. With this technology objects can achieve cloaking in the microwave range of the electromagnetic spectrum but they're still visible to the naked eye. Successful experiments in the microwave range indicates that we may be only a few years away from completing the same experiments in the visible light range. However, with present technology it's been difficult to engineer metamaterials that interact with radiation within the visible range. On the bright side, the underlying physics suggests that it should be possible granted the science of manufacturing metamaterials progresses.

The vast potential of metamaterials has prompted an entire new field of physics called **transformation optics**, which revolves around manipulating light for practical applications, often using metamaterials. Metamaterials are made of a lattice with a repeated pattern of inclusions that are smaller than the wavelength of the wave from which the object will be cloaked. Thus, radio or microwaves are easiest to experiment on since these waves have the longest wavelengths and have corresponding metamaterials that are easier to manufacture. Some properties of metamaterials such as the aforementioned phenomenon of the negative refractive index are not found in nature and may not even be possible using natural materials. It takes very precise manufacturing control to achieve a metamaterial with desired optical properties; developing a functional metamaterial cloak requires the combination and gradation of many refractive indices.

Limitations to current cloaking technology include:

1) The difficulty of broad-band cloaking. Typically cloaking is only achieved in a narrow band of the electromagnetic spectrum
2) Fabrication of metamaterials is still prohibitively expensive
3) Fabrication of metamaterials with features small enough to manipulate visible light is difficult
4) We can only cloak small objects. The squeezing and compaction of light rays disrupts the rays as they're steered around larger objects and creates artifacts that decrease effectiveness
5) Many methods of cloaking research are limited in viewing angle, observer position, or only work under water

Even with these limitations, the future looks bright. These hurdles are likely only transitory, as incremental improvements to fabrication technology and knowledge of metamaterials' effect on light should continually push cloaking research forward into the foreseeable future. The great promise of the nascent field of metamaterials is drawing a lot of researchers due to potential applications. This recent influx of brains and money should accelerate the velocity of advancement in the field.

SciFi Topic 3: Molecular Assemblers

Status of the technology: No working mechanical nanosynthesis machines have yet been built. Experiments abound and several blueprints for building such machines have been presented.

What to expect: Theoretically, building mechanical nanomachines that assemble molecules should be possible. Such natural machines like ribosomes exist in nature already. We can reasonably expect rudimentary machines to be developed by 2030 or 2040.

Typical reactions in a liquid or gas result after reactants come together via random thermal motion. A molecular assembler is a hypothetical nanomachine that could add structure and organization to this process by manipulating and creating molecules on an atomic scale. The reactants would attach to the assembler which would control the orientation and position of the reactants to catalyze a reaction. This already happens in the natural world. A ribosome is effectively a nanomachine that receives instructions from messenger RNA and uses these instructions to build the protein for which the RNA codes. The engineering challenge facing scientists is to use this biological inspiration to synthesize analogous artificial machines that can be programmed to build specific value-added structures at will. Like the ribosome, the molecular assemblers would catalyze reactions by juxtaposing reactive species and ushering in reactions.

Several blueprints have been developed to create molecular assemblers that would build proteins or other small molecules. One of the first goals may be to assemble diamonds by manipulating carbon atoms. Much early theoretical and peer-reviewed work focuses on building diamonds due to the crystal's simplicity, as it only contains one type of atom, carbon. A patent for diamond mechanosynthesis was even granted in 2010.

Scaling is proving a huge challenge. Scientists can already use scanning tunneling microscopes to move individual molecules around, but building anything useful would require moving hundreds to hundreds of millions of molecules around. Individual atoms and molecules are so tiny that the results from only a few molecular assemblers would be inconsequential for most uses. Thus a key attribute to the viability of this technology is that the assemblers can be programmed to self-replicate. Once a sufficient number of assemblers are made, they would then be reprogrammed to manufacture the desired product.

Applications of molecular assemblers would be nearly endless. Nanofactories consisting of armies of nanomachines would have the capability to build products that are precise down to the atom. Medicine, aviation, space, and warfare would be obvious beneficiaries of the technology, but atomically precise fabrication could be a revolutionary improvement to nearly every industry.

One risk is that the nanorobots would replicate themselves in an out-of-control fashion and consume all of earth's resources in an apocalyptic scenario. Since the molecular assemblers would be brainless, emotionless robots that operate by breaking apart raw materials to rearrange the atoms and replicate themselves, they could conceivably continue replicating until they ran out of resources. This low-probability but very high-impact scenario has been termed the "grey goo" and has gained notoriety in science fiction as a potential sequence of events that could end life on earth. Though the scenario is highly unlikely, the potential effect on humanity is so vast that experts in the field of nanotechnology will be taking necessary precautions and installing controls to prevent the accidental release of self-replicating nanorobots.

SciFi Topic 4: Force fields

Status of the technology: Scientists have found initial success in blocking matter using an electric force field. Blocking radiation like lasers is proving harder. Generating a sustained field like those shown in movies will be many years down the line if at all; nearly all current research is focused on generating quick, powerful pulsed fields.

What to expect: Expect commercial and space applications by 2040, then military application soon afterward.

Most of us have seen force fields in movies, television or video games at some point in our lives. The details differ; sometimes they're used on earth or other planets and sometimes in the vacuum of space, but they typically operate via energy or magnetic deflection and are transparent or translucent fields that can block bullets, lasers, or punches, and are sometimes used to detain prisoners. Are such force fields physically possible to create or are they purely a figment of science fiction?

Blocking matter and blocking radiation are two very different tasks. There is active research in both areas, and the research is generally split into developing energy shields that block one or the other, not both simultaneously. In general, teams across the world are finding more initial success in blocking matter.

There are a few initial prototype military armors that can flood the outer surface of a tank with a huge electric charge that creates an electromagnetic field with the capacity to repel or destroy matter. All methods developed so far are reactionary, meaning that instead of setting up a long-term force field to repel matter, the quick pulsed field is formed as a reaction to incoming bullets or charges.

Boeing was granted a patent in 2012 for a system that they developed that attenuates shockwaves and lasers via electromagnetic arc. Their system could be mounted on a vehicle and it projects plasma in an arc that blocks shockwaves upon sensing the incoming shockwave from an explosion. The energy barrier it generates can block enough of the shockwave to protect personnel inside the vehicle from injury.

Blocking radiation like lasers hasn't been successfully conducted yet, but mathematics and theory suggest that it should be possible to do so. The most attractive choice of material right now is to build an energy shield out of plasma. Success has already been proven naturally in the upper levels of the Earth's atmosphere, called the ionosphere. Plasma here blocks low energy radiation like radio waves. Blocking higher energy radiation like lasers would require a very dense layer of plasma. Lasers and other weapons would generally only constitute high energy radiation in the visible or ultraviolet range. The problem here is that blocking lasers would also block other radiation in the visible spectrum, so no light would pass through. The force field would blind the person it was protecting.

Thus, the key hurdles to building force fields are building a field that is constant rather than reactionary and building one that can block both matter and radiation. Generally, blocking matter is being attempted with electricity and blocking radiation is being attempted using plasma. Since we're still in the initial stages of building each of these, we're still a long way away from developing a unified field. Also, we would need to develop a field that doesn't blind or disable the person that the field is erected to protect.

So what can we *actually* expect for the future of force fields? Military technology will probably come after industrial and scientific applications. The Earth is protected from cosmic rays by the magnetosphere (essentially a natural force field providing radiation protection), but nothing protects the International Space Station or other satellites. An energy shield could serve a purpose in protecting scientists and equipment orbiting the earth in such satellites. Thus space programs have a vested interest in developing shields that block radiation. In fact, they're already pursuing the idea.

Prolonged exposure to radiation in space can damage DNA and cause cancer and neurological damage to the astronauts. The SR2S project, standing for Space Radiation Superconductive Shield, plans to create a magnetic force field using superconducting magnets to bounce harmful radiation away from satellites and astronauts. It can theoretically create a 10-meter wide field that can deflect rays away from a spacecraft and would be a big step in preventing injury and cancer from ionizing radiation and permitting prolonged space travel.

Sector 5: Transportation

Transportation Topic 1: Autonomous vehicles

Status of the technology: Billions of dollars in research money are being invested. Many conditionally automated systems are being honed and improved. Some companies have achieved full automation under specific circumstances such as suitable weather and a hand-mapped route.

What to expect: Within the next five years we will likely see automated ride-hailing in select cities. After several years of collecting data and assessing the safety and performance of these vehicles, automated vehicles for private sale will be rolled out, possibly around 2035.

We'll discuss the economics in more detail later, but the first companies to enter the inchoate autonomous ride-hailing or autonomous transport markets will likely dominate market share and stand to make monumental profits. This impetus is driving mountains of money into research and development of autonomous vehicles, both from established multinational corporations and countless startups. Google's subsidiary Waymo, General Motors' subsidiary Cruise, Tesla, Uber, Toyota, Honda, Ford, Volvo, Fiat-Chrysler, Nissan, Daimler, Intel and Samsung are only a few of the players developing and testing the technology. With all of this money and time being invested, self-driving vehicles are becoming increasingly sophisticated and there is no technological reason to believe that full unconditional automation can't be achieved. Thus, the question that remains is not *if* fully-autonomous cars will arrive, but *when*.

To standardize language and increase the accuracy of communication regarding autonomous vehicles, the National Highway Traffic Safety Administration and the Society of Automotive Engineers have created a gradation of five levels of autonomy:

- **Level 0. No automation**. The driver performs all tasks. For example, a Ford Model T.
- **Level 1. Driver Assistance**. Some features assist the driver who always must have control of the car. Such features include adaptive cruise control, parking assistance, collision avoidance, automatic lane centering, and other features that come standard on many new cars.
- **Level 2. Partial automation**. The car can take over certain functions such as steering, lane-keeping and acceleration/deceleration based on environmental factors. The driver must remain vigilant and at the wheel at all times. At this point, the driver can take his or her hands and feet off the wheel and pedals but must be ready to jump in and retake control at a moment's notice.
- **Level 3. Conditional Automation**. The driver must remain at the wheel but is not required to continuously monitor the environment. The driver may be requested to take control of the vehicle in times of uncertainty such as in construction zones or inclement weather. The car can read stoplights and street signs as well as change lanes without driver input. Some view this level of automation as controversial since it could lead to dangerous complacency, wherein the driver is unaware of the environment but may be asked to retake control of the car at a moment's notice.
- **Level 4. High Automation**. The vehicle can drive fully automatically under suitable conditions. At this level, no driver is required at all and an empty car could drive itself.

Roads must be well-mapped and in good weather and road conditions. A well-trained horse or horse-drawn buggy could potentially reach this level, though most horse-drawn buggies would fall at around a level 2.
- **Level 5. Full Automation**. The vehicle can drive fully automatically under all conditions. At this level, the car can drive on unmapped roads and even off-road. No driver or steering wheel are necessary.

As a recapitulation, a quick way to describe levels 1 through 5 are, respectively, "hands on", "hands off", "eyes off", "mind off", and "steering wheel unnecessary". In the discussion of the state of the industry below, I will periodically refer to level 3, 4, or 5 autonomy. You can flip back and refer to this list for clarification if needed.

Autonomy is achieved by using software to combine and process inputs from a multitude of sensors, plot a path, and then send instructions to actuators to control acceleration, steering and braking. Thus the two key technological challenges are to develop a system of fail-proof sensors that provide continuous high quality data about the environment and to develop smart software that will react promptly and properly to the incoming data.

In general, autonomous cars are equipped with about 8 cameras that together cover 360 degrees around the car, numerous ultrasonic sensors that detect close-ranged objects like curbs and parking obstructions, and forward-facing radar for long-range sensing. Many companies also opt to use lidar, which is similar to radar but uses light waves instead of the longer-wavelength radio waves.

There is a rift in the autonomous driving community regarding lidar. Lidar typically operates by spinning and shooting laser beams that scan the environment in 360 degrees and detect ranges to objects and vehicles. As such, these lidar instruments have a lot of moving parts, aren't durable, and are very expensive. However, it's the most powerful technology available in terms of quality of generated data; it can identify lane markings, edges of the road, and other objects that can be difficult for other types of sensors to detect.

Waymo believes lidar is necessary to achieve level 4 autonomy and up, but Tesla disagrees, claiming that it's too expensive and its incorporation would cause autonomous vehicles to be too expensive for much of the mass market. At $15,000 to $20,000 for a single lidar sensor, there's very little wiggle room to outfit the car with any other sensors and technology before the car is to be sold, if it were to target the mass market. Tesla intends to make an autonomy level 4 or 5 vehicle by foregoing lidar and instead integrating and combining the strengths of all remaining technologies such as ultrasonic sensors, cameras, and radar. Waymo is taking an alternate approach, as they decided to bring lidar manufacturing in-house and have developed their own lidar instruments for an internal cost of under $10,000. Additionally, they are testing new lidar technologies that don't require as many moving parts as the current instruments on the market. If improvements continue, in the next decade lidar may become cheap enough for economically feasible implementation into cars targeted to the mass market.

In addition to the aforementioned environmental sensors, autonomous vehicles are typically equipped with a GPS tracking system and internal sensors that can perform calculations based on conditions of the vehicle. These computations use data such as wheel revolutions and angle of the wheels in inertial measurement and odometry to calculate the position of the vehicle. The complimentary nature of combining this mathematical and GPS-based information with real-time sensor information creates a redundancy that will be vital to safety during full autonomy.

A suite of local and regional governments around the world have already given the green light to companies to test self-driving cars in their communities. However, the state of the research is at a bit of a crossroads. Many testing vehicles are around level 3 automation, which as briefly mentioned earlier is a dangerous and controversial level. Many research vehicles are only partially autonomous and may require the driver to take over in uncertain situations such as in a road construction area or in inclement weather. A person could be cognitively distant such as watching television and then be asked to take over the car with only a few seconds to react to a challenging environment. This quick, forced transition from computer to human has caused several wrecks already. Many researchers feel that this transition period of partial autonomy should be restricted to testing and that cars should not be rolled out commercially until they're 100% fully autonomous.

A key hurdle before wide-scale implementation of autonomous vehicles is likely to occur is to make them safer than their human-driven counterparts. The vehicles don't need to be 100% safe, but accidents and fatalities must be less frequent than those due to human error. In the United States, the current fatality rate is about 1 death per 1 million hours of drive time. Africa and Asia typically have slightly higher death rates and Australia and Europe slightly lower. Thus, this general level of death rate is the target for autonomous vehicles to beat. So far, this has not been the case, as self-driving automobiles typically require human intervention much more frequently than once every million hours of drive time. A key outlier here is Waymo. This company has not yet had an accident and they've logged over 10 million miles of road driven. Average human drivers would have crashed over 50 times in that number of miles. Though the achievement is impressive it must be qualified by the fact that the company has painstakingly hand-mapped the areas in which it has achieved level 4 autonomy.

Programming of the software is an incredibly challenging task. The vehicle cannot be told to simply follow all street rules at all times because many human drivers do not drive in this manner. Humans don't always follow driver's education rules and each person has developed his or her own idiosyncrasies and patterns to handle situations such as 4-way intersections and lane changes. It is paramount that autonomous vehicles are moderately aggressive to both "act" as human would expect a car to act, as well as to avoid a situation in which the car doesn't know what to do so it shuts down. Early research vehicles did just this at 4-way intersections; the cars were too cautious and weren't programmed with enough healthy aggression, so they shut down at intersections and refused to move. Such irresolute decision-making could be catastrophic if it occurs on a highway rather than at a simple 4-way stop.

In Arizona in 2018, a self-driving car killed a cyclist walking her bike in low-light conditions. All the hardware worked perfectly and identified the cyclist several seconds before impact, but the car's inability to identify the threat and predict her intentions resulted in the car hitting her without making an attempt to stop. Improvements in such decision-making under uncertainty will require many hours of machine learning training. On a positive note, the onboard sensors detected the woman while she was standing in the dark right next to the road several seconds before a human driver would have noticed her by visual cues. If engineers can solve the programming and decision-making issue, it's likely that the suite of onboard sensors will detect potential threats quicker and more effectively than human eyes alone, especially in low-light conditions.

Even with perfect hardware like sensor technology and computer vision, ethical questions remain regarding how to program the car to make decisions. For instance, should the car protect the driver at all costs? What if the car is careening towards a group of pedestrians who entered a crosswalk when they shouldn't have? Should the car veer away to hit a light pole, sacrificing the driver but saving 3 or 4 pedestrians? What if a collision with a bus of schoolchildren is imminent? How should the car respond? Questions like these indicate that programmers will be required to place relative value on human lives.

Once widespread level 4 autonomy is achieved, autonomous ride-hailing will become available. This will likely be the first major application of autonomous vehicle technology due to the expected profitability of the business model. Seeing these potential profits, technology companies are scrambling over each other to be the first to master the technology and enter the market. Each driverless car would be able to run 24 hours a day minus maintenance and refueling time. At current ride-hailing rates such as those charged by Uber and Lyft, it's not infeasible for a single autonomous car to make over $100,000 per year giving rides, likely recovering the entire purchase cost in less than a year. From this point on, the car will make nearly pure profit with very few costs for the company. It's likely that by the mid 2020's, electric vehicles will decrease in price to the point of becoming subequal to that of gas-powered cars, and they would require much less maintenance. Thus, these two technologies converging in the mid 2020's suggests that big cities may soon house fleets of fully electric autonomous ride-hailing cars.

Privately sold autonomous vehicles will probably become available several years after use in private ventures such as the aforementioned ride-hailing industry or the trucking industry. Once these private cars become available they could become an auxiliary source of income for the owner. Tesla plans to modify cars with safety and security features such as a locked glovebox and cabin camera that would permit people to let their car give rides and produce income while the owner is at work doing his or her 9-to-5 job.

A somewhat comical concern is that it'll likely be cheaper for electric cars to cruise rather than to pay for paid parking in city centers. Thus, some city officials are concerned that in the near future there may be thousands of riderless cars wandering city streets, cruising without purpose while their owners go about their business in the city.

Some optimistic tech CEO's will say that fully automated self-driving cars are just a year or two away. While it's true that Waymo has achieved level 4 autonomy in strict well-planned areas, widespread and safe autonomy is probably still at least 5 to 10 years away. Legislation has already been proactively passed in many areas to allow level 4 and 5 self-driving vehicles. Politics is not holding the technology back; the technological challenges are.

It would be indecent or even catastrophically dangerous to roll out sub-par vehicles with only level 3 or low level 4 autonomy. Many people already drive in a perfunctory manner, and giving them the option to take their eyes off the road only heightens their carelessness. The technology must be mature to be safe enough to roll out on a commercial scale, and the decision-making capabilities of the software simply isn't sophisticated enough yet. Likewise, critics and cynics raise security concerns regarding cyberhacking, jamming, and spoofing. Automation systems must be made resistant to outside illicit influence.

In sum, change is coming very soon. Some changes will be positive, such as fewer accidents and reduced traffic since autonomous vehicles could follow each other much more closely on the road than humans do. Other changes would be negative, at least in the short- to medium-term, such as the loss of millions of trucking jobs. In a decade the roads may look much different than they do today.

<u>Transportation Topic 2: Hyperloop</u>

Status of the technology: Decentralized research is being completed all over the world. Numerous prototypes and test-runs have been completed, typically on one mile-long tracks. Speeds around 250 miles per hour have been reached in tests.

What to expect: Virgin Hyperloop One has received the green light to build the first commercial Hyperloop in India, connecting the cities of Mumbai and Pune with planned completion by 2030. Other proposals and construction projects are likely to follow.

In 2012, Elon Musk proposed the term "Hyperloop" for his particular vision and blueprints for a novel mode of public transportation consisting of a magnetically levitating pressurized pod being propelled through a sealed tube partially evacuated of air. Concepts for various evacuated tube transport technologies had been proposed previously by others so the idea wasn't entirely without precedent, but his fame and media hype have led to the term Hyperloop largely becoming a generification of the concept of the vactrain, or vacuum tube train, as a whole.

The science behind the concept is simple, though the engineering is proving to be a challenge. Pressurized and vacuum pneumatic tube systems have been used since the 1800's to transport solid objects like packages and such systems still see use today in some drive-through banks to transport documents and cash between the car and teller. The key difficulty facing the Hyperloop is the sheer scale of the proposed projects.

The two key factors that limit the speed of traditional vehicles are air resistance and friction between the wheels and the ground. The Hyperloop assuages both issues. The track is proposed to be an enclosed and air-tight pipeline that would be largely evacuated of air, greatly reducing air resistance. The pods would be levitated and thus would not experience physical friction with the track. Levitation would be achieved either using air bearings, which is the technology behind air hockey puck and hovercraft levitation, or by the more popular idea of using superconducting magnets. This decrease in resistances would permit the Hyperloop to theoretically reach speeds much greater than traditional trains. Original proposals claimed that the pods would reach speeds of over a thousand miles per hour, but more recent and realistic estimates target the 700 mile per hour range. Even at this speed, the Hyperloop would beat airliners and bullet trains to claim the title of the fastest mode of public travel.

Original designs for vacuum tube trains typically envisioned pods operating in a total vacuum, but the reality is that achieving and maintaining a full vacuum over hundreds of miles of track is quite difficult and expensive. Leaks anywhere along the hundreds of miles of tubing could stop the system from working properly. As a result, more modern proposals like the Hyperloop propose a low-pressure system that could withstand small leaks rather than a total vacuum. For the Hyperloop concept, air pressure in the tube would be 1 millibar, which is equivalent to flying 200,000 feet above sea level, or $1/1000^{th}$ of atmospheric pressure at sea level.

Routes for a Hyperloop have been proposed in countries all over the world. One of the most popular is Los Angeles to San Francisco, which was Musk's original planned route to roll out the technology. This 6-hour drive would only take around 1 hour in a Hyperloop. However, it's highly unlikely that this will become the first active route. In August 2019, the first Hyperloop was permitted to proceed with construction in India between Mumbai and Pune, typically a 4 hour long, 150-kilometer drive. At a proposed top speed of 700 miles per hour, total trip time would be reduced to under 30 minutes. Construction is set to begin in 2020, and completion is planned before 2030. A few more obstacles need to be overcome; after constructing the first small section, safety certifications and approval will be required to continue toward completion of the project.

Hyperloop research is very decentralized. Many private companies, startups, and college research teams around the world are independently working to push the technology forward. Test tracks have been built all over the world to facilitate experiments on various aspects of the pod or track.

Funding will assuredly be a huge impediment to the technology. Building hundreds of miles of specialized pipeline along with ancillary equipment to maintain vacuum and power would require massive initial capital. At $50 million to $150 million per mile, projects can easily reach into the billions of dollars.

Land development and land use is another factor that will make translating the technology from the lab to market a challenge. The technology is viewed as a way to connect huge city centers, and most proposals for routes reflect this, as Hyperloop stations are typically proposed in city centers next to other existing transport infrastructure. Building a huge new infrastructure asset in an existing city would be a nightmare of real estate development and eminent domain disputes. To make matters worse, the Hyperloop would be required to maintain very low turning radii since it would be moving so fast; otherwise the g-forces would be very uncomfortable for passengers. Thus, it would be difficult to avoid obstructions as it travels between two cities and would instead likely cut through mountains, vineyards, or other sensitive uses of land. While constructing an elevated track directly alongside existing infrastructure such as highways and railroads may partly ameliorate the land acquisition issue, I don't envy whoever has the job of securing rights to construct along those hundreds of miles of land.

Lastly, many safety and security concerns are still unanswered. Since the tubes are held in a partial vacuum they could theoretically implode upon being damaged by earthquakes or terrorism, though teams advancing the technology are aware of this concern and are taking steps to avoid catastrophic failure. In case of accidents or emergency malfunctions, how will exits be completed? The pods contain pressurized breathable air but the tube is mostly evacuated of air and likely won't have many emergency exits. These concerns will need to be addressed as the technology inches closer to becoming a reality.

Putting everything together, the main hurdle for the technology isn't scientific or technological. The hurdles arise from civil engineering and scaling challenges, politics, economics, and safety and security concerns. With all of these unanswered concerns and downsides, it's worth exploring whether pursuing a Hyperloop is worth the time, money and effort. The Japanese superconducting magnetically levitating train SCMaglev can reach 370 miles per hour and it doesn't require the energy cost, danger, and capital expense of a pressurized tube. The maglev is already a proven technology and theoretical calculations suggest that improvements to maglev technology can get them to speeds of 500 miles per hour in the future. The SCMaglev is much like the Hyperloop, minus all the additional costs. Is the Hyperloop a big enough step over current maglev trains to justify investment of billions of dollars, or would we be wiser to instead fund research into furthering hydrogen-powered superconducting maglev train technology?

Though it's still unclear whether the Hyperloop will become a reality, it would be nothing less than revolutionary for urban living and for industry if it does indeed materialize. People would no longer need to live near the city where they work. A person could live in a city 300 miles away from his or her work and still have a 25 to 30-minute commute.

Sector 6: Biology

<u>Biology Topic 1: De-extinction, also known as resurrection biology</u>

Status of the technology: Proven technology. An extinct animal (European goat) has already been cloned. The hurdles going forward are not technological; they're ecological, ethical, and economical. That being said, we would only be able to resurrect species that have died within the past 100,000 years. Anything older would be nearly impossible.

What to expect: We can expect a single mammoth to be resurrected as a vanity or conservation awareness project, but the first entire self-sustaining population of a species to be resurrected will likely be a small, fast-reproducing extinct animal like the passenger pigeon. We can reasonably expect this to happen by 2040 – it depends on when scientists can secure funding and when they can get past the red tape.

In May of 2013, Russians found a nearly perfectly preserved 4,000 to 10,000 year-old wooly mammoth carcass frozen on an island near Siberia. It still had blood and muscle tissue, almost as if it were preserved in a deep freezer. The scientific world was abuzz with thoughts of using cells from this specimen to clone mammoths and resurrect the species, and the finding has kindled new interest in the field of resurrection biology. But is it possible to de-extinct entire species?

After an animal dies, its DNA degrades rapidly over time. The half-life of DNA is just over 500 years. In a few hundred thousand to a few million years, there's nearly nothing left. Dinosaurs went extinct about 66 million years ago, so with current scientific knowledge and technology, creating a real-world Jurassic Park is impossible. Dinosaurs are so old that any soft tissue has turned to rock; there's no DNA left. However, reviving animals that died more recently such as saber-toothed tigers and giant ground sloths could be feasible.

There are three main approaches to resurrecting extinct species: Cloning, genetic reconstruction, and backbreeding.

To use the **cloning method**, scientists must have frozen cells from the extinct species available. This method was used in 2003 to resurrect a Pyrenean ibex, a European wild goat that went extinct in the 1990s. Since the animal went extinct so recently, scientists had frozen cells from previously living specimens available. They used the same nuclear transfer method of cloning that was used to clone Dolly the sheep in 1996. The scientists injected nuclei from frozen ibex cells into goat eggs that had been evacuated of their own nuclei. These eggs were then implanted into living female goats, who carried the ibex to term. Though the ibex died within a few minutes after birth, it was born alive, a proof of concept for the first attempt to revive a dead species or subspecies.

In **genetic reconstruction**, scientists must have access to hair, skin, or any other genetic material from the extinct species. From this sample, the genome will be sequenced. Once the genome is known, scientists would find a closely related animal and cut and paste sections of extinct-species DNA into the extant relative's stem cells until they arrive at the DNA of the extinct animal. Then the stem cells could be reprogrammed into egg and sperm cells and used in cloning.

Backbreeding is artificial selection, where breeders selectively breed for ancestral genes to attempt to bring them out. This is the most low-tech way to "resurrect" old species but it has already been done by several research groups around the world with initial success. This method isn't true resurrection, since the goal is to achieve a visually similar animal, but physiologically and behaviorally they might be very different than the extinct animal.

The auroch is the extinct giant cow-like beast from which the modern cow was bred. The Tauros Programme is an international program based in the Netherlands to identify auroch genes in cows and to breed cows to recover those genes. Once the breeders arrive at a sufficiently auroch-like animal, they plan to release some into the wild, reclaiming the territory aurochs roamed before they went extinct in 1627. Auroch DNA is available from various fragments in museums, which has allowed scientists to sequence their genome and compare it to modern cows'. The program has realized success thus far; their cows look very much like cave paintings of aurochs as well as scientific recreations of aurochs from skeletons. However they're not *really* aurochs. They're cows bred to bring out their ancestral auroch features.

There's a similar backbreeding program in South Africa called the Quagga Project that intends to breed zebras to resemble the extinct zebra relative, the quagga, which went extinct in the 1880's. The program began in 1988 and by the mid 2000's has achieved quagga-like zebras. The group hopes to return quagga-like zebras from the project back to the quagga's former natural habitat.

Now back to the mammoth. Fortunately, mammoth tissues have been preserved well enough that a variety of different methods could be used to resurrect the species:

1) **Cloning**. The nucleus from a mammoth cell could be inserted into the nucleus-evacuated cell of an elephant, which could be inserted into a living female elephant for gestation.
2) **Repeated insemination** of elephants with sperm from a frozen mammoth. In a few generations, elephant DNA would be diluted and an almost pure mammoth would result. Since elephants don't reach sexual maturity until 10

to 15 years of age, this technique would take decades to complete.

3) Since the mammoth genome has been mapped, **genetic reconstruction** could be used. The Asian elephant would serve as the base DNA, and chunks of mammoth DNA would be inserted to replace some of the elephant DNA.

4) **Backbreeding** of elephants is an option, but this method isn't nearly as sexy as the other methods and would only result in a mammoth visually, not genetically. Like method 2 above, this technique would take decades to complete since several elephant generations would be required.

We can see that the hindrance to resurrecting the mammoth is not technological. Computer algorithms can reconstruct the broken mammoth DNA and cloning technology has come a long way since Dolly the sheep was first cloned in 1996. We have many technologies at our disposal to resurrect the mammoth from the materials on hand. Instead, we haven't revived it due to economical, ecological, and ethical concerns.

Economical

Resurrecting a single animal is great for publicity and proof-of-concept but it doesn't restore the species long-term. For a population of animals to survive, the gene pool must have genetic diversity. Genetic bottlenecking leaves the animals susceptible to disease or infertility. It would take hundreds or thousands of individuals to make a healthy, genetically diverse population. Thus, a large amount of money would need to be dumped into any true species resurrection project to birth as many individuals as possible and from as large of a variety of individuals as the scientists can get their hands on.

Ecological

Every species has a role to play in its ecosystem. Since the ultimate goal of a resurrection project is to release specimens into the wild, humanity needs to critically question whether releasing a new player into an ecosystem is a good idea. Would the new animal outcompete native animals? Tundra animals and plants are now well-suited to their current ecosystem without the mammoth. Would placing hundreds or thousands of new hairy 5-ton herbivores in the tundra disrupt the ecosystem?

Another question is whether the extinct animal's old ecosystem is still around. Humans are urbanizing and deforesting more land each year. Should we even attempt to resurrect a species that went extinct due to human activity? It's probable that we would have little native habitat with which to release the animal where it would have high long-term survival prospects.

Ethical

A substantial argument against resurrecting extinct species is the fact that species are still going extinct every day, and that the money and time that would have gone to de-extinction could have been better spent towards conservation and habitat protection of living endangered animals. It would take millions of dollars to revive an extinct species, but there are thousands of currently living species near the edge of extinction that could use resources to keep their struggling populations alive.

On the flip side, research into de-extinction is translatable into conserving extant species. The same methods described above could be used to increase the genetic diversity of the gene pool and aid in conservation of critically endangered species. The California condor, Javan rhino, and Sumatran tiger would all be good candidates on which to practice these methods and to add variety to their DNA and make their tiny populations bigger and stronger.

The Future

A single mammoth may be revived soon as a proof of concept or vanity project, but the first large-scale full species de-extinction project will likely be the passenger pigeon. Humans recently hunted them to extinction and put a hole in their ecosystem. The pigeons helped control forest underbrush to prevent fire hazards. The passenger pigeon is closely related to the band-tailed pigeon, which makes it a great candidate for genetic reconstruction. We could edit the band-tailed pigeon DNA by inserting passenger pigeon DNA. The bird's quick life cycle would allow us to make hundreds of individuals at a fraction of the cost of reviving an equivalent number of a larger species.

<u>Biology Topic 2: Abiogenesis, the origin of life</u>

Status of the research: General scientific consensus is that RNA-based life arose from stagnant pools of water rich in organic materials, and DNA-based life subsequently evolved from those RNA-based ancestors.

What to expect: Scientists will continue fleshing out the smaller details, like how cells arose and where on earth this may have occurred.

How did life originate? It's a huge question that has invoked everything from gods to aliens in various cultures. In scientific circles, the challenge is to explain **abiogenesis** – how did life originate from non-life?   The earliest known organisms are microbes from around 4 billion years ago. Their fossilized remains don't offer much in the realms of morphology or physiology, so the only quality evidence they offer is the time in earth's geological history when life began. Science is focused on elucidating the events that happened around this time to birth life, and existing theories involve deep-sea hydrothermal vents, volcanoes, viruses, radioactive beaches, self-replicating lipids (fats), and life originating several kilometers below earth.

The most popular theory and now nearly a scientific consensus is that life arose from "primordial soups", which were warm ponds or puddles of water containing amino acids. The most likely scenario is that all life today descended from RNA-based ancestors borne in the soup. A huge breakthrough in the theory came in 1952, when scientists created amino acids, the building block of proteins, by electrically zapping environmental chemicals like methane, ammonia, hydrogen, and water vapor. These laboratory experiments suggested that energy from lighting or radiation in a natural environment can create the chemicals needed for life, and the ancient "primordial soup" would have contained these amino acids. These soups would have been localized in certain areas with high energy inputs such as hot shorelines, swamps, and hydrothermal vents.

Origination of life requires several steps to occur, and passionate disagreements still occur regarding the details and the sequence that these occurred:

1) Origination of the ability to replicate
2) Origination of the ability to self-assemble
3) Origination of cell membranes
4) Origination of DNA and/or RNA

Science usually operates on the **principle of parsimony**: the simplest explanation is most likely to be correct. Current life is very complicated, involving coordinated interactions of DNA, RNA and proteins. There's a "chicken and the egg" type of problem: DNA needs proteins to replicate itself and proteins need DNA to code for themselves. In short, DNA needs proteins and proteins need DNA. How could this situation have arisen spontaneously? The simplest answer lies in RNA.

There's an explanation that involves a simpler precursor system to the aforementioned DNA-RNA-protein system. It involves an intermediate step: RNA-based organisms. RNA can store the genetic code and carry information like DNA and has the added benefit of self-replication. However, it can also fold up into active shapes to usher in and catalyze reactions like proteins, bond amino acids together into proteins, and perform other work that proteins do. In short, it can effectively perform most of the tasks that both DNA and protein do, at least at a perfunctory level. The current prevailing theory is that all current DNA-based organisms evolved from RNA-based life forms that were biochemically simpler.

These hypothetical RNA-based organisms would begin with simple self-replicating RNA molecules evolving before proteins or

DNA. The next stepping stone would be ribonucleoproteins (RNA bound to proteins working together), and then stand-alone proteins. The ribosome, the component of cells in modern animals that reads the genetic code and forms proteins from it, is a ribonucleoprotein. It's quite possible that this organelle may be a remnant of the RNA-based organisms of the past. DNA is more stable and durable than RNA, which would explain why it would have eventually replaced RNA as the information-storing molecule. While RNA can perform some of the functions of proteins, RNA is formed from only 4 different bases whereas proteins are formed form 20 different amino acids, so proteins have far more variety and are thus more diverse and versatile. An analogy can be drawn here to letters of the alphabet: RNA only has 4 different "letters" to choose from when coding for a molecule whereas proteins have 20. This increased flexibility and diversity would explain why proteins have mostly replaced RNA in catalyzing reactions and doing most other work in a cell.

There is no shortage of theories on the details of how each of the four steps above happened. The scientific community now generally agrees that simple RNA-based self-replicating entities were the first living things, arising sometime around 4 billion years ago. The exact details of how and where this occurred is still hotly debated. As mentioned in the opening paragraph, theories invoke everything from lightning to volcanoes to deep-sea hydrothermal vents.

One fun hypothesis is called **panspermia**. The panspermia hypothesis speculates that life arose somewhere else in space and arrived on Earth on meteorites or through another cosmic event. However, this explanation does nothing to explain the origin of life, it just shifts the question of the origin of life elsewhere. Space, including asteroids, has a lot of organic molecules and amino acids. The chemistry necessary for life isn't restricted to earth, so this theory is not as far-fetched as it first sounds.

We'll have to stay tuned and observe where scientists' research takes the field. It's hard to predict whether the field will stagnate or if scientists will soon make a breakthrough through paleontology, laboratory testing, or through theory. There still remain many unanswered questions.

Chicken and the egg

While that finishes up our discussion of the origin of life, I'd like to now explore a quick digression regarding the chicken and the egg problem referenced above: the "problem" does indeed have a solution. About 300 million years ago, a group of animals called amniotes evolved a hard-shelled egg that allowed them to lay the eggs on land without the eggs drying out. Prior to this, all eggs were soft and had to be laid in water or the eggs would dry out, much like the fish and amphibians eggs of today. The evolution of the hard-shelled egg was quite a huge development that severed the reliance of the animal lifecycle on water and permitted the rise to most land-dwelling groups of animals that we know today like reptiles and birds. Dinosaurs evolved from hard-shell-laying amniote ancestors about 240 million years ago. Birds, including chickens, evolved from dinosaurs.

So what came first, the chicken or the egg? The answer is the egg. Red junglefowl, the wild bird native to Southeast Asia from which humans domesticated the chicken, evolved less than 50 million years ago. Modern chickens were only domesticated around 10,000 years ago. So the hard-shelled egg is 300 million years old, and the chicken is either 50 million or 10,000 years old, however you want to define it. The chicken slowly but directly evolved from ancestors that were already laying hard-shelled eggs.

<u>Biology Topic 3: Head transplant</u>

Status of the technology: Experiments on animals have had mixed successes and failures. Contemporary ethical norms dissuade the type of research that has occurred in past decades, such as scientists stitching together a 2 headed dog or researching how long a decapitated dog head could be kept "alive". No full-blown head transplant has been done yet on either animals or humans.

What to expect: Most experts agree that we're nowhere near ready to try the procedure on humans. However, a few scientists are confident and want to attempt the procedure very soon. We can realistically expect the procedure to occur possibly by 2030 somewhere with lax regulations like China, and we can also expect the first procedure to go very poorly.

To some, head transplantation is the holy grail of modern medicine. Successfully performing the procedure would earn the surgeon a spot in history books. There is not only a suite of technical challenges to performing the procedure, but also a number of regulatory and ethical issues to navigate. We'll start with the science and then get into the ethical considerations.

There has been a surprising amount of head transplantation research done on animals, such as rats, monkeys, and especially dogs, starting as early as 1908. In the 1920's and 30's Russian scientists decapitated dogs and hooked their heads up to pumps to keep the blood pumping and keep them "alive" for an extended period. The severed heads could respond to stimuli such as sound and touch, often for over an hour. A few decades later in the 1950's, a Russian scientist stitched one dog's head onto another dog to make a 2-headed dog. The closest we've gotten to a human experiment was a head transplant that was performed on a corpse in China, but this is a far cry from an *in vivo* procedure.

A key hurdle is the fact that there's no clear stepping stone to performing a head transplant. Surgeons and patients must take a giant leap of faith and fully commit to attempting the first procedure. The most likely scientist to be the first person to complete a head transplant is an Italian doctor named Sergio Canavero. Dr. Canavero nearly conducted a head transplant on a live human in 2015, but the wheelchair-bound man who originally volunteered to have his head placed onto a brain-dead organ donor body backed out before the surgery could be performed.

The following is Dr. Canavero's general game plan. He first plans to find a patient with a healthy head but a faulty body, such as a muscle-wasting disease or other debilitating disease of the body. With this person's consent, he would decapitate the person and put his or her head onto the headless body of a person who was brain-dead but whose body was otherwise "healthy".

As far as the procedure itself, Dr. Canavero would begin by chilling the patient's head down to 10 degrees Celsius to minimize the brain damage. Then he'll cut all the skin around the neck to expose the muscles. The muscles will be color coded so they could be matched up with the similarly color-coded muscles of the donor body. Everything but the spinal cord will be cut and then the head will be drained of blood to prevent blood clotting. Severing the spinal cord is the last step in the decapitation process. The surgeons would use a diamond-edged blade to make an incredibly smooth and clean cut. The steps are reversed to put the head on to the donor body. The spinal cord would be the first thing to be reconnected, using polyethylene glycol "glue", a substance used in printing ink and skin creams. Then the blood vessels, trachea and muscles would be connected, then finally the skin. Following the procedure, the patient would be kept in a coma for several months to allow the incisions to heal and the spine to fuse. It is estimated that the procedure would take around 30 surgeons and over 24 hours to complete. What could possibly go wrong?

From a technical viewpoint, there are three main challenges to the procedure:

1) Transplant rejection. However, with modern powerful immunosuppressant drugs, this challenge can be overcome
2) Brain damage due to insufficient blood flow and hence oxygen. To combat this, the surgeons would form two teams that would operate simultaneously to hopefully decapitate each person at nearly the same moment and move very quickly to attach the head.
3) Properly lining up and connecting the spinal cord. This is by far the biggest challenge. Neurons don't only control movement but also pain and many other biological functions. Any error during the procedure could result in the patient living a lifetime of agony or paralysis.

What are the philosophical, ethical, and legal implications?

Regarding philosophy, if you had a head transplant would *you* still be *you*? It's tempting to think that your memories would follow your head wherever it goes, but recent research on a group of flatworms called planarians suggests that reality may not be that simple.

If you cut a planarian in half, it'll regrow a new body on each half. Even if you make a transverse cut to cut its head entirely off it'll regrow a new head. Research on these organisms suggests that they can retain some memories after losing their head and regrowing a new one. Researchers trained some planarians to perform tasks that are not normal planarian behavior, cut off their heads and allowed them to regrow it, then tested whether they would retain the unique behaviors. The planarians retained the memories of their training. Thus, for them, some memories are stored elsewhere, perhaps in the neurons outside of the brain? Are the results of studies on worms even partially transferrable to humans? The answer is that we simply don't know yet. Flatworm research is obviously a far cry from human research, but my point here is that it's not outside of the realm of possibility that the brain doesn't hold all of a person's thoughts and memories. Could memories from the donor transfer to the new brain?

Regarding ethics, is it moral to subject a brain-dead donor's body to this risky procedure when his or her donor organs could have instead been used to save 3 or 4 other lives? Who qualifies for the procedure and under what circumstances would experts allow the procedure to proceed?   This is all uncharted territory at the moment.

Regarding legal and administrative issues, who has legal rights to the new post-procedure person? Is it the head, the body, or both? It seems logical that the donor head would be the new legal person.   In other transplants, a faulty organ is removed and replaced with a good one. Here, the head is the good part and the body is faulty, so it really should be called a body transplant. Of course, the courts may have a differing opinion.

Another legal question arises if the person has children post-transplant. The person's mind would *presumably* be his or her own, but his or her genetics as far as egg and sperm production are concerned, would be that of the donor body. What would happen if the donor-body's family makes claims to the kids, with whom they share family DNA?

There is no higher-risk medical procedure. The slightest accident or peccadillo could result in catastrophic consequences, and nothing can fully prepare the doctor for the first procedure. If you had a body-wasting disease, would you volunteer your head?

<u>Biology Topic 4: Human Enhancement</u>

Status of the technology: Human enhancement technologies are here. Plastic surgery, contact lenses, external hearing aids, surgically implanted cochlear hearing aids, pacemakers, orthodontics, blood transfusions, organ donations, weight training and dietary supplements like creatine for physical performance and ginseng for cognitive performance are already widespread and socially acceptable. More controversial enhancements like fetal abortion based on DNA testing for genetic disease, prosthetics controlled by electrodes implanted into the brain, implantation of electronic devices for medical diagnostics or communication, and using DNA editing as treatment for disease are gaining acceptance.

What to expect: As we will see below, technologies borne from research into treating disease is often directly transferrable to improving already-healthy humans. There is often a very fine line between treatment and human enhancement. Technology will inevitably proceed forward and human enhancement will slowly become more accepted.

Opposition to radical technological advancement is to be expected and is not a new phenomenon. When writing was established over two millennia ago, Greek philosopher Socrates was quoted in his staunch opposition to written word, "it destroys memory and weakens the mind, relieving it of work that makes it strong. It is an inhuman thing." He also maintained that words are not a complete representation of knowledge, and that words are to knowledge as pictures are to their subject. In short, Socrates preferred oral communication and thought that written word would atrophy the mind since it reduced the need for one to draw details from memory. Socrates walked the walk too; almost everything we know about him was in fact written by his student

Plato rather than Socrates himself. Though it's natural and often healthy to share Socrates' skepticism of new technologies, if we were always afraid of progress we'd be stuck in the stone age.

Blood transfusions, organ donations, uranium enrichment, using phenol to sterilize surgical equipment, moving from representative currency to fiat currency, *in vitro* fertilization, Norman Borlaug's cross-breeding of wheat... all of these advancements were met with criticism from either the general public at large or from distinct and outspoken groups worried about public safety or the long-term implications of the technologies. A certain degree of skepticism is assuredly healthy and any new technology should be thoroughly evaluated by experts to determine whether the benefits outweigh the risks. Today, many people are afraid of new technologies like smart glasses, synthetic blood, gene editing, brain electrodes, and drone technology for a variety of reasons, chiefly privacy and safety concerns. The success of potentially invasive future technologies are often contingent upon the acceptance and success of once-novel technologies that would be transitional in retrospect. For instance, commercialization of smart contact lenses are largely reliant on the success of precursors like Google Glass, and creating designer babies by DNA editing is reliant on the acceptance of using DNA editing technologies for therapeutic purposes such as curing Huntington's disease or cystic fibrosis.

Speaking of DNA editing, does the thought of directly editing the DNA of living humans get a visceral reaction from you? It very well may. Human augmentation is a topic that inexorably polarizes people, and DNA editing is one of the most visible and debated topics within the field. Both within the scientific community and within the general public, you can find plenty of people who wholeheartedly support the idea of using technology to make minds sharper and bodies stronger than what is naturally possible, as well as plenty of people who are diametrically opposed to the idea.

In fact, the subject of exceeding natural human limits has produced many entire books of its own. Debating human enhancement naturally leads to conversations about the idea of transhumanism, which is the philosophy that humans can evolve past its current or natural physical and mental limitations. Advocates of transhumanism believe that humans should make cutting edge technologies available to the mass population in order to enhance humanity's collective physical and mental abilities. If this were to materialize, decades down the line enhanced humans would be so superior to modern humans that they would be discretely distinguishable from natural humans and could be classified as post-humans.

Transhumanism has been around for decades and at first was only a futurist thought experiment, but now it's creeping closer to reality every day. As will be explicated below, people's innate desire to improve themselves combined with the fact that the line between treatment and enhancement is so blurry creates a scenario where society will almost certainly slide toward social acceptance of direct germline DNA editing and other technologies to enhance themselves and their children.

Before we get into the science, let's ask ourselves a philosophical question: why should the limits of nature be a limit for us if we have technology available to improve upon nature? Are nature's boundaries arbitrary? This is where some people may invoke religion by claiming not to "play god" with humans or not to alter humans since they have been created in the image of a deity. However, others support the claim that these limitations of our natural gene pool are arbitrary and thus improving upon these limits presents no moral quandary. Below is a thought experiment on the limitations of human eyesight.

LASIK eye surgery is a widely commercially available tool for semi-permanent vision correction. The 30MM+ total patients that have undergone the surgery since its inception demonstrate that people are willing to go face to face with knives, needles and lasers to improve themselves. The benchmark goal for LASIK surgeries is to achieve "normal" vision, 20/20. 20/20 vision means that, at 20 feet away, you would be able to see objects with the same visual acuity that most people could see at 20 feet away – thus "normal" vision. What if a surgical implant became available that could provide 20/5 vision. 20/5 vision means that, at 20 feet away, you would be able to see objects with the same visual acuity that most people would have to be only 5 feet away to see. If you had perfectly healthy 20/20 vision, would you undertake the surgery to implant the device? Is there an ethical difference between a legally blind person undergoing surgery to achieve 20/20 vision and a healthy 20/20 person seeking surgery to achieve 20/5? Would it be immoral to seek out the surgical implant?

The same analogy can be drawn for color vision. Scientists have created glasses that allow colorblind people to see the full spectrum of visible light containing all colors that normal people can see. If they created glasses that could see outside of the visible spectrum such as the ultraviolet and infrared ranges, would you wear them? I'm sure you would, but how about undergoing surgery that would allow you to see into the ultraviolet range like birds, exceeding the limits of natural human ability?

These are examples of the slippery slope alluded to earlier. The hypothetical surgical eye implant or color-enhancing eye surgery are only two examples, but across many fields of medicine similar issues arise where "treatments" are available that can surpass the regular human condition. For a real-world example, double below-the-knee amputee and Olympic sprinter Oscar Pistorius, also known as the "Blade Runner", was met with criticism in 2007 by the International Association of Athletics Federations, who claimed that his springy carbon-fiber prosthetics gave him an unfair advantage over competitors with natural feet and ankles. This resulted in a back-and-forth court battle which Pistorius ultimately won, but during the proceedings doctors tested his running biomechanics against normal sprinters and discovered that the prosthetic limbs used significantly less energy than natural feet and required less mechanical work to lift the body. If mid

2000's-era prosthetics could meliorate a double amputee's performance so drastically that he could operate on a subequal or superior level to the top athletes on Earth, imagine the unfair advantage 2020's-era devices could impart not only on an amputee, but also if utilized by a fully healthy individual.

For amputees, scientists have created bionic prosthetic limbs with artificial electrodes that sense muscle activations in the residual limb stubs. The nerve signals that activate what's left of the muscle in the stub originate from the brain and travel down the spinal cord and to the residual limb. Tiny computers in the prosthetic decode the nerve signal to produce an intended action. Scientists have succeeded in creating brain-to-computer harmony, but computer-to-brain harmony remains to be achieved; specifically, the amputee cannot yet feel what the bionic limb is touching. The ability for the limb to input information to the user's nervous system to "feel" what the limb feels would be a leap forward in bionics. Right now, bionic limbs are only tools for amputees; they're not yet a fully integrated part of the person. Successful bi-directional communication between brain and computer would advance the field to a new level. Research teams around the world are working on such bidirectional communication. Research on microchips implanted into the brain that allow paraplegics to control appendages are paving the way for other human/brain experiments and to close the brain-residual limb-prosthetic loop with a bi-directional flow of information.

A popular method to connect paraplegics to a bionic limb is to use an agonist-antagonist myoneural interface. In short, this basically means surgically connecting two antagonistic muscles to an electrode. Antagonistic muscles are opposites – when one contracts, the other flexes. For instance, the biceps flex the lower arm whereas the triceps extend the lower arm. Likewise, the hamstrings flex the lower leg whereas the quadriceps extend the lower leg. These are both examples of agonist-antagonist pairs of muscles. When surgeons connect both muscles to an electrode, they can recreate the natural process of muscles signaling their status to the brain. When an agonist contracts, it stretches the antagonist. The antagonist alerts the brain that it's being stretched, which helps the brain deduce the position of the extremity. By harnessing information provided by both muscles in the pair together, scientists hope to be able to more accurately relay information back to the brain, which is lacking in the current generation of prosthetics.

This research into bionic prosthetics is directly transferrable to creating increasingly sophisticated exoskeletons. By directly linking the human to electrodes and a strong machine exoskeleton, possibly by using agonist-antagonist pairs as mentioned above, we may be able to jump higher, run faster, and lift many times more weight than humans can now. We could even control and feel structures not found in natural humans. By using these techniques originally developed for prosthetics research, we could theoretically connect and control virtually anything with our brain – wings, hooks, tentacles, claws, flippers... the sky is the limit. The bi-directional brain-computer interface is the immediate goal; once we achieve this duality of information flow, the doors will open for many advancements in bionics.

Most humans in the developed world are connected to computers, phones, and the internet at nearly all times and these devices all vastly improve mental and cognitive function. A trend we can expect moving into the next few decades is for technology to migrate from outside of our bodies to being on and then inside of our bodies. The first step is to move computers and other devices onto the human (e.g. wearable devices, smart watches, smart fabrics and augmented reality glasses). Next, they will move inside the human (e.g. brain electrodes, smart contact lenses, and implantable diagnostic microchips that can detect levels of blood chemicals and disease).

For many people in the developed world, a personal cellphone is by his or her body for virtually the entire day, often never more than an arm's reach away. It's the first thing most people check in the morning immediately after waking up. Cellphones are almost already an integrated part of us. As a society we're already accepting of pacemakers. Thus, at least for the noble purpose of the pacemaker, having an electronic device implanted within us is acceptable. MIT has developed interactive tattoos that may represent a transitional step before implantable leisure devices. These tattoos can be controlled much like a touchscreen on a phone. The person can touch and interact with the tattoo, typically on his or her forearm. The tattoos can track health and generate near-field communication signals. Near-field communication has a range of only a few inches, but it could be used for a variety of digital currency payment, electronic ticket and identity provision uses. The tattoo may potentially partially displace phones and swipe cards in the future.

And now on to the biggest and most divisive issue: DNA editing and genetic engineering. For a little background, genetically engineered foods have been commercially available since the Flavr Savr Tomato went to market in 1994 with altered DNA and had a longer shelf-life than natural tomatoes. In the years since this pivotal moment, many more genetically modified foods have entered the supply chain and society, as a whole, has become more accepting of genetically modified foods. The editing of humans remains a whole different story.

All DNA editing is not made equal. Cells in the body can be categorized into two types: gametic cells and somatic cells. Gametic cells are the sex cells in the body – the egg and sperm. DNA edits made to the gametic cells will pass down to the next generation. Somatic cells make up the majority of your body's tissues and mass -- basically everything besides the eggs and sperm. DNA changes made to somatic cells will <u>not</u> pass down to the next generation. Predictably and understandably, gametic cell DNA editing is far more controversial than somatic cell DNA editing, as gametic cell DNA editing will permanently alter the person's entire future genetic line.

Gene editing has been around for decades but techniques have historically been expensive, had low success rates, and low precision. This all changed with the discovery of CRISPR-CAS, a precision DNA editing technique derived from a natural antiviral immune system in bacteria. While CRISPR-CAS was first discovered in 1987, its enormous scientific and commercial potential wasn't realized until the early 2010's, when research on the technology exploded around the globe. CRISPR-CAS operates with nearly 100% precision, has dropped the price of gene editing by over 95%, and has cut the timescale of gene editing experiments from years down to weeks.

CRISPR-CAS could be used as a therapy for HIV, cancer, and other diseases by altering and augmenting the DNA of one's own immune cells, rendering them more efficient at targeting a specific malady. Alternatively, it could allow scientists to directly target hereditary diseases by repairing faulty DNA. Genetic diseases that CRISPR-CAS could rectify include cystic fibrosis, Huntington's disease, sickle cell disease, colorblindness, fragile X syndrome, and hemophilia. In particular, diseases caused by an impaired single gene, like cystic fibrosis, fragile X, sickle cell and Huntington's, would be very straightforward to treat. There are upwards of 10,000 single-gene genetic diseases that would be great targets for a CRISPR-CAS-based therapeutic.

Using CRISPR-CAS on reproductive cells means that the edits will be passed on. With the technology, we could potentially make irreversible changes to the gene pool of humanity. This exact same technology that could rid humans of tens of thousands of diseases could also be employed to target genes responsible for height, intelligence, and other human traits.

It's difficult to overstate the potential impact of CRISPR-CAS. With the technology, humanity bears an enormous burden to use it morally and ethically. Scientists now have near god-like power to alter germ-line DNA, the DNA that is passed down from generation to generation, with surgical accuracy. One could potentially edit live cells or switch genes on and off with minimal expense. Designer babies, superhuman strength, and potentially extended lifespans are now on the table.

People in many developed countries have the option to conduct tests on early fetuses for a variety of diseases and have the choice to abort fetuses with major defects before the pregnancy progresses past the first or second trimester. Down syndrome, for instance is one of the simplest and most widespread ailments to be tested. The disease can be reliably diagnosed non-invasively via ultrasound and blood test, and the fetus is often terminated when it's discovered. More extensive tests are both possible and available through a procedure called an amniocentesis, which screens the amniotic fluid surrounding the fetus. Amniocenteses can detect spina bifida, cystic fibrosis, other genetic diseases, and fetal infections. Thus in certain situations, people are pre-selecting babies based on medical conditions.

Humanity has already begun the next step past simply choosing to terminate pregnancies of progeny with undesirable conditions. More specifically, the path toward designer babies largely stems from advancements in assisted reproductive technology to overcome infertility. *In vitro* reproduction involves the isolation and fertilization of eggs which can later be implanted and incubated to term. With the parallel advancements in diagnostic tests to screen embryos for major hereditary diseases, in *in vitro* fertilization doctors are now able to selectively choose an embryo that does not have a testable disorder, or even to choose an embryo with desirable genes. This gene selection is a primitive form of designing a baby. By combining these technologies with CRISPR-CAS gene editing technology, we could theoretically directly edit the genome of prospective babies before implantation. People could select not only to avoid genetic diseases, but also to select for hair color, eye color, and even disposition for criminal behaviors or cognitive ability.

The first few designer babies will likely be altered to eliminate genetic diseases. Slowly, as people become more de-sensitized to the process, more and more questionable edits will go through. It's entirely possible that the moral backdrop may shift from being against gene-editing toward the thought that <u>not</u> removing undesirable traits is unethical because it denies children a cure when one is available. However, if any type of selection no longer becomes voluntary but instead becomes state-mandated, even for a noble cause such as editing embryos with Huntington's disease, one could make the argument that it would lead us on a path toward eugenics. This isn't quite as implausible as it may seem at first; a growing number of European Union countries are making vaccines mandatory. If a country mandates prophylactics for infectious diseases, is the thought of compulsory prophylactics for hereditable diseases really that farfetched?

A dichotomy exists regarding the permissibility of altering vanity traits. On one hand, choosing for things like eye color and hair color serve no therapeutic purpose and may be forbidden. On the other hand, choosing for eye color and hair color doesn't hurt anybody, and thus should be at the discretion of the parents. I suspect that vanity traits will initially be off the table but will slowly creep in. Traits like metabolism and visual acuity can be boosted but are in the grey area between the medical arena and vanity. It's possible that traits like these would serve as a transition between rote medical therapies and rote vanity altering. Only time will tell how this unfolds.

Here's another thought game similar to the LASIK and eyesight discussion earlier. Is it ethical to use CRISPR-CAS to treat an embryo with Fragile X Syndrome but not to augment a normal embryo? In other words, is it ethical to edit an embryo to bring his or her projected intelligence quotient up 40 points from mental retardation (say, an IQ of 60) to an average IQ of around 100? If this is indeed ethical, is it then ethical or unethical to edit a normal embryo to give him or her the exact same 40 IQ point boost, from average (IQ = 100) into the range of "very superior" or "genius" (IQ = 140)? This is a question that humanity's moral collective must face and decide upon in the coming years.

Aging is also a huge topic in the field of human augmentation. While aging is due in part to cumulative damage to cells, there are also genes that directly affect aging and these can be altered by genetic engineering. The life extension movement has some fiercely dedicated advocates and has spawned several non-profit organizations like the Life Extension Advocacy Foundation and startups like Calico Labs and Human Longevity, all dedicated to extending human life past humanity's current limit of around 120 years. Early research suggests that slowing down aging is almost assuredly possible and that stopping or even reversing aging is not out of the realm of possibility.

More visionary ideas exist for immortalizing humans further into the future. The Alcor Life Extension Foundation has a vault of over 100 bodies that they keep frozen with liquid nitrogen. Those who bought a spot at Alcor hope that technology will progress to such a degree in the future that they will be able to be thawed and reanimated. An alternative to reanimation in human form is mind uploading, where a person's consciousness and memories are transferred to a non-biological computer. Science still has a long way to go regarding mapping the brain before this venture could become reasonably possible.

Now for a quick foray into ethics. Critics raise the concern regarding the various technologies discussed above that society's collective ethical and moral judgement will be delayed. That is, science will advance past the point of no return and by the time we realize our mistake it'll be too late. DNA editing could have gone awry or the control of brain electrodes could be in the hands of militants or an evil corporation. At this point society's collective conscience would like to ban or revert these technologies but it would be too late.

Another ethical quandary is the price point and accessibility of the new technologies, namely germline DNA editing. If the price of DNA editing renders it reserved for the rich, it's plausible that mankind could experience rapid human evolution, but only for those who could afford it. By editing the germline DNA, the rich could iteratively optimize each generation of their children's genes for superior cognitive and physical abilities. In the future, we could see a world of genetic castes ruled by a genetic elite that are superior in every way to normal humans.

Will DNA editing even be an ethical issue in 100 years or will transcending the boundaries of natural human nature be the norm? It's impossible to say. Either way, given the influential power of many current technologies in development, it's imperative that we proceed slowly, pondering input from all major stakeholders.

In sum, we find ourselves in exigent circumstances. Humanity has critical decisions to make within the next decade regarding what level of human augmentation is allowable on the legal, regulatory, moral and ethical fronts. That being said, the natural causality arising from the fineness of the line between treatment and augmentation suggests that progress toward augmenting humans will assuredly continue despite any heavy-handed regulatory or legal hurdles. A pretty scary thought, if I do say so myself.

Sector 7: Physics

Physics Topic 1: Room Temperature Superconductivity

Status of the technology: In the research phase.   Room temperature superconductivity has not been achieved yet. The record so far for highest-temperature superconductivity is around -70°C.

What to expect: It's uncertain when we should reasonably expect room temperature superconductors or if room temperature superconductivity is even possible.   The factors underlying superconductivity are so complex and poorly understood that it's difficult to predict how quickly the research will proceed. My unfounded assertion is that we might achieve room temperature superconductivity around 2070, though I may likely be decades off in either direction.

In electrical conduction, materials allow electrons to pass through them.   Conductive materials like copper, silver and aluminum are used in electronics, power distribution and other applications in which electrons need to be shuttled from one place to another.   As electrons move across the conductor, they experience some resistance and lose a slight amount of energy to light, heat, and sound. This is why electronics often heat up when in use.

A **superconductor** is a material in which electrons can flow freely without resistance.   When electrons flow through a superconductor they don't lose energy. Such superconductors have immense usefulness. Superconductors would allow for 100% efficient electronics, faster supercomputers, more economical MRI machines, levitating transportation, and smaller desktops and other temperature-sensitive equipment since they wouldn't require bulky heat sinks and cooling systems. Scientists can create superconductors in a laboratory setting, but since most need to be cooled to nearly absolute zero, practical applications are nearly nonexistent thus far. It would require a vast amount of energy and infrastructure to roll out superconductor applications while the current state of the technology still requires that the material be cooled to the temperature of deep space. Thus, the discovery of materials that have superconductive properties at room temperature would be a momentous breakthrough.

At present, about 6% of electricity from power plants is lost to the grid before it gets to the end user. Six percent may not seem significant at first, but extrapolated over millions of homes and businesses it's a great deal of wasted energy. If engineers could instead construct the grid out of superconducting wires then essentially nothing would be lost to heat and utilities could get electricity to end users at a lower cost to both the customer and the environment. Of course here I'm making the bold claim that some of the savings from the improved logistics would be passed on to the customers.

Definitions of high-temperature superconductivity vary, but the threshold is often stated as either above 30K (-243°C or -405°F), which is a value established during early descriptions of superconductivity in the early 1900s, or 77K (-196°C or -321°F), which is the boiling point of liquid nitrogen. For the common folk it doesn't matter which definition is used; what matters is whether materials can superconduct near room temperature ($\approx$293K, 20°C or 68°F).

The general idea behind materials gaining superconductive properties at colder temperatures is that there are fewer thermal vibrations at these temperatures that decrease efficiency by inhibiting flow. When the material is so cold that its vibrations have nearly ceased entirely, the electrons can flow more smoothly and without interruption. Most metallic superconductors are only superconductive below 30K and thus must be cooled with liquid helium. Some newer "high" temperature superconductors are superconductive up to around 138K (-135°C or -211°F) and can thus be cooled with liquid nitrogen instead. While a great step in the right direction, this is still somewhat of a far cry from room temperature.

So far the highest temperature scientists have demonstrated superconductivity was 203K (-70°C or -94°F), reached by using a hydrogen and sulfur compound. Achieving this experimental feat required pressure of over a million times atmospheric pressure, around the pressure in the core of the Earth. While achieving such pressures is not practical in industrial or commercial applications, experiments like these are vital to explicating the underlying science of superconductivity. The property of superconductivity itself is a conundrum; researchers generally don't know what mechanisms are giving certain materials their superconducting properties. In fact, it's one of the major unsolved mysteries of condensed matter physics. Luckily this challenge has drawn in resources from around the world to aid in elucidating the issue.

Since the nanoscale factors contributing to superconductivity remain a mystery, researchers hoping to create high-temperature superconductors find themselves in a quandary. How can they make better superconductors when they don't know what qualities of the materials need to be improved? Some of the best high-temperature superconductors to date are layered materials, which are very complex and have many factors at play. For instance, promising compounds are typically complex mixtures such as bismuth-strontium-calcium-copper-oxygen, yttrium-barium-copper-oxygen, iron-arsenic, or hydrogen-sulfur.

Explanations for the processes that give rise to superconductivity abound. There are many esoteric terms that follow because I wanted to at least briefly mention some of the multifarious theories and schools of thought in the field to underscore the uncertainty of current scientific knowledge. Theories for the processes that permit superconductivity include the pairing of electrons and nucleons, pairing of magnetic fluctuations, binding and pairing of electrons, or the specific geometry type and symmetry of the pairing of electrons. Another explanation is antiferromagnetism, the phenomenon where the magnetic moments of neighboring atoms are always opposite of each other. This contrasts with regular ferromagnetism, where the moments all align in one direction. Yet other explanations invoke interactions of the wavefunction, which describes the quantized system as a set of probabilities. In short, there are many possible explanations for the underlying phenomenon. These specifics will need to be worked out before humanity can master the engineering of superconductors.

The future of high temperature superconductivity is uncertain, but simulations and theoretical predictions suggest that, once improved, uranium hydride may have superconducting properties near room temperature. Alternatively, predictions suggest that substituting some of the sulfur atoms in sulfur-stabilized metallic hydrogen with phosphorus atoms and increasing the pressure further than a million atmospheres may also achieve room temperature superconductivity. Time will tell whether either of these predictions reflect reality. Whether the experiments work or not, continuing these types of extreme experiments slowly pull back the curtain on the underlying principles of the phenomenon and are vital to further our quest to achieve practical superconductivity.

Physics Topic 2: Dark matter

Status of the research: Due to observations of the gravitational effects of interstellar objects, we know that dark matter exists, but that's about the extent of our knowledge. We don't know much about the granular properties, but the most popular current theory is that dark matter is made of weakly interacting massive particles (WIMPs). Most research is focused on elucidating whether WIMPS exist in the cosmos.

What to expect: If dark matter is in fact made of WIMPS, we should expect to find them by 2025. Scientists have set up numerous experiments all over the world to find them and are actively searching. If the WIMPs theory is incorrect and dark matter is instead made of something else, its properties will likely remain a mystery for several decades.

Everything we experience is only a tiny fraction of reality. Our perceived reality, including planets, stars, and everything else that we can see or feel makes up only 5% of the universe. The remaining 95% of the universe is invisible to us, and scientists are still theorizing and experimenting to determine the composition and properties of what comprises this balance. What we do know is that 27% of the universe is accounted for by an exotic concept called **dark matter** and the remaining 68% is accounted for by an even more enigmatic concept called **dark energy**. Dark matter will be described here, and dark energy will be discussed in a separate entry that follows.

In our Solar system, the planets closest to the Sun move faster than those further away. For instance, Mercury is zooming around the sun at a blistering 105,000 miles per hour. Earth is moving at 67,000 miles per hour, Mars at 54,000 miles per hour, and Neptune at a leisurely 12,000 miles per hour. This trend is a manifestation of Kepler's Second Law of Planetary Motion and the decrease in orbital velocity of objects at the distal edges of the system is both typical of and expected in a system of bodies orbiting around a heavy central mass.

Galaxies usually center around a heavy massive object in the middle such as a black hole. Thus, we should expect to see a similar pattern to what we observed on a smaller scale in the Solar System example: stars close to the center of the galaxy should orbit very quickly, whereas distal stars should orbit the galaxy's center at a slower pace. In practice, we observe the opposite; distant stars usually rotate at equal or higher speeds than those near the center. Galaxies don't act as typical systems with a big mass at the center. Adding the mass from stars producing observed starlight into the calculations doesn't help to explain the orbital speeds and trends either. To make the math work, scientists need to add in decentralized mass (not all in the center). Since galaxies don't abide by Kepler's second law, we can conclude that they can't be modeled as a system with mass concentrated at the center; in contrast, much of the mass of the system must be located near the outskirts of the galaxy. This is one of the key observations and reasons for believing dark matter exists. By adding invisible mass into the calculations scientists can model galaxies to recreate the orbital speeds that are seen in empirical observations.

There's more to the story than simply the speed of the orbits. The gravity of the normal matter alone is not enough to form the galaxies we see. If there was no dark matter, the stars would instead be more dispersed and not form galaxies. There's something in and around galaxies that doesn't interact with light but keeps the entities together. The mass of galaxies is essentially constant throughout the disc, not concentrated in the middle and dropping towards the edges. In fact, some galaxies seem to have a halo of mass near their outer edges.

There are several other reasons for believing dark matter exists. The details are beyond the scope of this book but I'll mention them briefly. These include, but are not limited to, studies of:

1) Gravitational lensing, which is the way that massive objects bend light
2) Temperature fluctuations and peaks in the cosmic microwave background radiation
3) Supernova observations and the implication on the acceleration and energy density of the universe

In short, there are many corroborating reasons to believe not only that dark matter exists, but that it exists in a roughly 5-to-1 ratio with normal matter, as per the fitting of calculations and simulations with empirical observations. Where do scientists go from here? So far gravity measurements are the only thing they've measured that offers any clues to the identity of this peculiar substance. It doesn't seem to interact with the electromagnetic spectrum, which is the basis for most astronomical instruments to make observations. How can scientists determine the properties or composition of dark matter?

One way to learn more about dark matter is to create a big list of what it *could* be and then start crossing things off the list:

1) We know dark matter is not simply clouds of normal non-light-emitting matter because it would emit particles we can detect. We do not detect particles originating from dark matter.
2) It's not antimatter because antimatter produces gamma rays when it collides with normal matter, and we don't detect that.
3) It's not black holes. Black holes are violent places that warp space-time, but dark matter is scattered more evenly all over galaxies.

Gas, dust, rogue planets, and dead stars have also been eliminated as explanations. In large part, all the "normal" explanations have been crossed off and only bizarre or exotic explanations remain.

Since dark matter interacts with gravity but not light and there's a lot of it, the prevailing theory is that it's likely made up of a particle that we haven't discovered yet. Elucidating the properties of the prospective new particle is not a trivial task, since it doesn't interact with light, which is a standard property scientists use to observe other particles. We expect the new particle to have mass but to only weakly interact with other known particles. Scientists have conducted a variety of experiments to positively detect dark matter but all attempts have failed so far.

Experiments all around the world are currently looking for weakly interacting massive particles (WIMPs) because discovering these will likely mean that they have found dark matter. Though the WIMPs theory is the simplest answer to amalgamate mathematical and observational data, experiments have been unable to detect them so far and some experiments have been going on for over two decades. Due to this prolonged stagnation, there's currently a transition in the scientific community toward exploring other options, such as other new particles with properties other than those of WIMPs, entire new fundamental forces, or extra dimensions of space.

Scientists are attempting to detect WIMPs through a variety of methods. Since theory suggests the particles can pass through earth, one method is to measure flashes of light or recoils from interactions when dark matter particles strike a pool of atoms buried deep in the earth's crust. Scientists cool the system to near absolute zero and use detectors to look for the scintilla of energy that would occur if anything crashed into the system, which is typically comprised of a pool of argon or other otherwise inert material. An alternative method is to create dark matter directly by transiently producing it in particle accelerators. Lastly, other scientists are scouring space, searching for two dark matter particles colliding and annihilating each other which may result in a release of energy such as gamma rays, something we could theoretically observe.

Other researchers are using a mathematical or theoretical rather than experimental approach. They seek to modify general relativity; perhaps Einstein's theory works well on the scale of our solar system but not at a galactic scale? Some such mathematical theories have been invoked, which modify our current understanding of gravity to explain the extra gravity we see in galaxies, but without the need to include the effects of dark matter.

In sum, it's tough to predict what will come of dark matter research. Even primary researchers in the field don't know what to expect in the next 5 years, let alone further into the future.

Physics Topic 3: Dark Energy

Status of the research: Mathematical models and measurements of the expanding universe strongly suggest dark energy's existence. No direct experimental observations have been made.

What to expect: Unless scientists realize an unexpected breakthrough, the nature of dark energy likely won't be elucidated until the late 2030s or beyond.

As I'm sure you noticed from reading the previous entry on dark matter, scientists know next to nothing about dark *matter* other than the fact that it exists. Yet we know even less about dark *energy*.

For starters, scientists are not sure if dark energy is an entity of its own or instead simply a property of empty space. Either way, dark energy can be thought of as the energy that resides within empty space. Its density is much lower than ordinary matter or dark matter, but since it's uniform throughout the vast expanse of space, it comprises around 70% of the mass-energy of the universe. The energy density of dark energy is so tiny that it's overwhelmed and has negligible interactions anywhere that normal matter or dark matter resides.

Measurements of astronomical phenomena such as the cosmic background radiation, supernovae, shifting of light from distant galaxies towards the red end of the visible spectrum, and gravitational lensing all suggest that the expansion of the universe is not constant, but accelerating. The accelerating universe combined with the standard model of cosmology and general relativity together steer scientists to speculate on the existence of dark energy.

The 70% value mentioned earlier as the percentage of the universe that's comprised of dark energy comes from equations derived from Einstein's theory of general relativity and from measurements of the cosmic background radiation that suggest the universe is mostly flat. The Friedmann Equations are equations based off Einstein's theory of general relativity that can predict the geometry of the universe based on the ratio of the observed mass to a calculated critical mass. To get the flat universe, observed and critical density need to be equal. To reach the critical density, 70% of the critical mass needs to be accounted for by something else other than normal matter and dark matter. The prevailing theory is that the missing mass-energy of the universe is dark energy. Various spacecraft observations of the cosmic background radiation have corroborated this estimate, approximating the dark energy anywhere between 68% to 73% of the mass of the universe.

Dark energy can be thought of as reverse gravity, but much weaker. Gravity pulls objects together, but dark energy pushes them apart. Dark energy does not get diluted as space expands. As the universe expands, more space phases into existence as well as more dark energy. This means that the density of dark energy remains constant even as the universe expands. Thus, dark energy seems to be created from nothing. One theory is that dark energy could be the energy from virtual particles phasing into and out of existence in empty space. "Empty space" may not actually be empty; it may have its own energy, though small.

Like dark matter, dark energy interacts only with gravity which makes it extremely difficult to observe, experiment on, and study. It has no electric or magnetic interactions. Its density is negligibly tiny, so it's virtually impossible to measure in laboratory experiments. All other forces and interactions dwarf any potential actions of dark energy by orders of magnitude. The reason dark energy comprises so much of the mass in the universe is because it permeates the entire universe and fills otherwise empty space, of which there's an unbelievably large expanse.

The future of dark energy research is quite uncertain. Probing dark energy will take high precision measurements of the acceleration of the expansion of the universe to find out if and how the acceleration changes over time and space. Besides these empirical observations, much research either remains purely theoretical or hinges on ongoing concomitant research on dark matter.

Some scientists are attempting to modify general relativity to include provisions for both dark matter and dark energy. A subset of these theories attempts to merge dark matter and dark energy into one entity. The unified entity could either exhibit properties of both dark matter and dark energy at once, change over temporal or spatial scales, or dark matter could decay into dark energy.

Though thought games have engendered a variety of alternative explanations for the data, the simplest explanation is that dark energy is simply a fundamental property of space. Even within this paradigm exists competing theories. The cosmological constant theory of dark energy states that it's an *unchanging* property of space. In contrast, the quintessence theory of dark energy suggests that it's a field that can *change over time* and can be either attractive or repulsive, depending on its ratio of kinetic and potential energy.

In sum, we know very little about dark energy, other than the fact that its existence is suggested by mathematical models and large-scale observations of the acceleration of the expansion of space. It's likely that the granular properties of dark *matter* will be elucidated before scientists see much progress in understanding the nature of dark *energy*.

<u>Physics Topic 4: Quantum Computing</u>

Status of the technology: Right now we can think of quantum computers as being in a similar stage as to where classical computers were in the 1950's: giant room-sized monsters that take an army of Ph.D.'s to operate. Functional quantum computers have indeed been created but they are not yet as fast and versatile as conventional computers. At present, the goal of research in the field is to demonstrate **quantum supremacy**, i.e. showing that quantum computers have the capability to solve problems faster than conventional computers. This has not been shown yet, though various companies hint or claim that they have achieved or will soon achieve the goal.

What to expect: Quantum computers have the potential to shift the computing paradigm, but skeptics see quantum decoherence, error-proneness and noise as too large of hurdles to overcome and thus suspect that quantum computers will never live up to the hype. It's uncertain what to expect. If researchers can mitigate the problems currently plaguing quantum computers, we might see them being used industrially by 2035 or 2040. If research does indeed progress, we can expect them to be used mostly for big data projects rather than day-to-day use, as the ability to crunch numbers on unfathomably huge datasets is the main advantage quantum computers exhibit over conventional computers. On the other hand, if the aforementioned hurdles truly are too tough to overcome, we may never see practical applications.

The progress of shrinking computer parts is about to meet its physical limits. Much of the increase in computer speed in the past 50 years has resulted from our ability to fit ever-increasing numbers of transistors onto an integrated circuit chip. The scale of some of the smallest transistors is approaching the size of a single atom. Transistors act like a gate to block or allow the flow of electrons, and today are on the order of only a few nanometers in size. At around 7 nanometers in size, an effect called **quantum tunneling** can occur, in which electrons teleport across to the other side of the transistor, rendering the gate ineffective.

Since quantum properties are beginning to interfere with the improvements scientists are attempting to make in computers, the scientists hope to instead leverage these quantum effects to their advantage with the advent of quantum computers.

Quantum computers use a wholly different system of making calculations when compared to traditional computers. Traditional computers use **bits**. When the transistor is blocking the electricity, the bit reads a zero. When the transistor allows electricity, the bit reads 1. In contrast, quantum computers use **qubits**. Qubits are not controlled by electricity, but rather the spin of an electron in a magnetic field or the horizontal or vertical polarization of a photon. Until the qubit is read, it can be in superposition, meaning it can be in both states 0 and 1 at once. The qubit will lock in on a value once we attempt to read it.

As an example, three regular computer bits can store one piece of data out of 8 (2^3) total combinations:

000, 001, 010, 100, 011, 101, 110, 111

Three qubits in superposition, on the other hand, can store all 8 different combinations at once, in parallel. This can be thought of as a certain probability of being in each state, with the sum of all eight probabilities equaling 100%.

Scaling this up, it becomes apparent that this represents a massive improvement in memory storage. 20 qubits can store over a million different combinations of data at once, but 20 regular bits can only store *one* piece of information out of the million different combinations.

Traditional computers use logic gates to perform calculations and operations on bits, and everything is discrete and binary. Quantum computers, on the other hand, use quantum gates instead of logic gates. Engineers can use quantum gates to manipulate, entangle, and superposition qubits before measuring an outcome. Entanglement means that changing the properties of one qubit can change the properties of another, even if the two qubits are not next to each other, and superposition, as mentioned earlier, means that a qubit can be in multiple states at once. Once a measurement is made, the superpositions collapse into singular values.

Contemporary quantum computers have to be cooled to colder than deep space to function properly. Thermal vibrations and environmental fluctuations can cause the computations to fail. Thus, if quantum computers become available on the market, they'll likely be targeted for specific industrial and commercial purposes unlike the general purpose personal computers of today. What we're likely to see is coordination with regular computers rather than pure quantum supremacy and replacement of traditional computers. We simply don't need the massive data-crunching capability of quantum computers for most day-to-day tasks, so quantum computers will likely never fully supplant traditional computers, at least not for many decades. What will probably happen is that there will be a few quantum computers that can be used on a time-share basis on the cloud.

Quantum computers will be useful anywhere enormous data sets are being manipulated. This includes simulations, information technology security and cryptography, web searching, climate models, and creating new drugs via computer models. The theoretical capability of quantum computers to quickly crack encryptions that would take years for classical computers is what currently peaks the interest of governments around the world. Quantum computers have the potential to serve as tools to break in to other countries' encrypted networks.

Several non-trivial problems bedevil quantum computing research:

1) High noise and error proneness. Determining quantum states is based off of probability amplitude through a mathematical interpretation of the system called the wave function. Since the quantum computers are making calculations based on probabilities, error checks and multiple agreement must be built into the system to have confidence on the final output.
2) Quantum decoherence occurs when entanglements between the system and the environment or other interactions transfer quantum information to the external environment. Cooling the computer down to near absolute zero can assuage but not eliminate this issue.
3) Measuring the superpositioned states of the qubits and collapsing them to a single value is another critical point that can introduce error.

Output from a quantum computer is typically given to a certain probability. The confidence in the result is increased by repeatedly initializing the data and running through the quantum gates, outputting the result several times.

In 2019, IBM released Q System One, which is a quantum computer that was developed for "commercial use", though it's not actually ready for sale. IBM essentially streamlined and packaged a quantum computer into something that externally looks like a regular computer. This may be a step forward, but I wouldn't say it's a leap forward. Usually quantum computers take up a great deal of space since most of the computer must be cooled to near absolute zero temperatures to minimize vibrations and must be shielded from the outside environment as much as possible. Q System One is no exception; it's about the size of an entire room: 9x9x9 feet.

Various companies like Google, IBM, and Tsinghua University in China have recently come forward to claim quantum supremacy but their results are being tested and verified by other groups. In short time, we should know whether quantum supremacy has been achieved.

<u>Physics Topic 5: Time crystals</u>

Status of the research: Proof of concept complete. Two time crystals have been created, one at the University of Maryland and one at Harvard.

What to expect: Research into time crystals is still in its infancy so it's not entirely clear what applications may be possible. The top contender is for data management in quantum computing; we could perhaps expect to see this application by 2050 or 2060. I must qualify that the uncertainty in this prediction is great.

The **symmetry of space** dictates that if you do a science experiment in your kitchen, you should be able to repeat that experiment in your neighbor's kitchen, in a different city, or in a different country. It shouldn't matter where you are as long as all the relevant parameters (humidity, temperature, etc) are the same. Regular crystals have a peculiar property where they break this nearly universal property of the symmetry of space. As we will elaborate in the next paragraph, the way crystals organize as they form means that they aren't the same in every direction. This unique property of crystals resulted in scientists predicting that a 4-dimensional crystal might be possible. Follow-up experiments were able to create 4-dimensional time crystals and confirmed the theoretical predictions.

Salt crystals, ice crystals, and other regular crystals all exhibit a repeating pattern in 3-dimensional space. The crystal has a regular structure that's determined by the atoms that comprise it. For instance, table salt is made of positively charged sodium atoms and negatively charged chlorine atoms that organize themselves into a neat and repeating pattern that maximizes the exposure of each atom to neighbors of opposite charges. The pattern is regular: positive, negative, positive, negative.

However, the pattern that salt crystals take differs depending on the angle at which you look at it. As an analogy, think of blue-lined ruled paper. Going from top to bottom, you see a repeating pattern of blue, white, blue, white, but going left to right, you'll either be on a white line surrounded by two blue lines or on a blue line surrounded by two white lines. Many crystals have a similar structure. Looking from one angle you'll see alternating sodium and chlorine atoms:

sodium → chlorine → sodium → chlorine → sodium → chlorine

However, if you look in another direction you might see:

sodium → sodium → sodium → sodium → sodium → sodium

And this line of sodium atoms will be surrounded on each side by a row of chlorine atoms, much like the horizontal pattern we see in blue-lined ruled paper.

This directional difference that we see in crystal patterns is formed in completely random and symmetric space. For instance, you can precipitate crystals from a solution of salt water by dangling a string in it. Directional, structured order arises from the complete randomness and homogeneity in the salt water. That is, no matter where you are in the salt water, everything looks the same in every direction. This ability for crystals to break the symmetry of 3-dimensional space resulted in a physicist by the name of Frank Wilczek to predict in 2012 that the periodicity of crystals could continue into the 4th dimension: time.

The idea is as follows: since regular crystals have a repeating pattern in space (in three dimensions), time crystals would have a regular, repeating pattern in four dimensions (space and time). The time crystal would sit in one configuration for a while, then flip to another configuration, then flip back, in a repeating pattern.

Since time crystals would be in a stable (lowest-energy) state, they would continue oscillating forever. This sounds impossible at first -- in many minds it immediately brings up questions like perpetual motion and conservation of energy.

Scientists were in fact able to create time crystals within only a few years after the idea was conceived. Most matter is in equilibrium and motionless at its resting state, that is, it doesn't move unless you introduce some type of energy to it. Time crystals are the first non-equilibrium matter humans have ever created; they're like jello perpetually jiggling with nothing poking it. It wiggles and oscillates at its resting state:

Time crystal: configuration A → configuration B → configuration A → configuration B

Thus time crystals break **time symmetry** and locally breaks the conservation of energy. But what are the implications?

If you flip a coin, what are the chances it lands on heads? 50%. What if you wait 10 minutes and flip it? 50%. What if you wait an entire year then flip it? 50%. Time is nearly universally symmetric. A time crystal's property of the breaking of time symmetry would be like having a 50% chance of heads now, then a 60% chance of heads and 40% chance of tails if you wait 10 minutes before flipping.

Time crystals are still so novel that scientists are not sure what potential practical applications may be possible in the future. It will be a long time until they find any practical application. However, two main ideas have been put forth. First is timekeeping. Time crystals oscillate at a reliable frequency, so they may be useful in keeping time more accurately than any methods currently available. Second is memory storage for quantum computing, but huge advances on both the quantum computing front and the time crystal front are necessary for this application to manifest.

To summarize, the periodicity of regular crystals breaks spatial symmetry. The extension of this concept into the 4th dimension, time, is the time crystal. Time crystals oscillate between configurations and repeat through time.

Sector 8: Miscellaneous Technologies

Misc Topic 1: Blockchain

Status of the technology: Proven technology. Its most popular and widely used application is serving as the infrastructure for cryptocurrencies.

What to expect: We can expect to see continued application of blockchain in cryptocurrency but also applications in supply chain management and general data management in the next few years. The technology is a quick and secure way to store and track data, so any industry that requires recordkeeping and data tracking could potentially find use.

At its core, blockchain is a safe and secure way of writing down records that is resistant to tampering or modification. Those records can be anything: monetary transactions, invoices, accounting entries, contract validation, securities and commodities trading, tracking and supply chain, sales, digital music downloads, transfers of goods, transfer of digital assets like video games, online voting, and ownership of virtual pets, to name a few. If you can write a transaction or record on a notepad, you can write it on a blockchain.

As an analogy to how blockchain works, imagine being in a grocery store with 50 other people. Everybody in the grocery store has their own notebook and they write down any transactions that occur in the store. Now, let's say that you get hungry and decide to buy a Red Bull, a Snickers, a pack of Oreos, and a family sized bag of Doritos, which comes out to $20.

To buy the items, you give the cashier $20 and announce to everybody in the store that you're making the transaction. They all agree that you did indeed give the cashier $20 and he did indeed give you your groceries. Everybody writes down in their own notebooks that you bought $20 worth of groceries. After you're finished paying, the lady behind you buys the $30 worth of gummy bears in her shopping cart and she announces her transaction to everybody. Again, everybody in the store agrees that the transaction is valid and each person adds the transaction to their notebooks. Everybody in the store will always have the most-up-to-date listing of all transactions that have occurred.

Now, let's also assume that the cash register is broken or not being used. Thus, the record of the transactions occurring in the store is limited to the people's collective notebooks. In this scenario there is no central authority deciding what transactions are valid, more specifically, no cash register. Peer concurrence among the other shoppers is what decides on the validity of each transaction. Agreement on the validity of a transaction must occur before everybody logs the transaction into his or her notebook. Likewise, no single person has the "main" record. Everybody always has an equally legitimate and updated copy of the record of transactions occurring in the store.

Transparency is vital to the integrity of this system. The security relies on the fact that everybody can see what transactions are occurring and which transactions are agreed upon as valid. This system would be quite difficult to hack. If you wanted to hack the system, you can't just change one entry on one person's notebook. Everybody else's records would contradict your fake entry and you'd be overruled. Thus, the replication of the latest data by all people helps to ensure the accuracy and quality of everybody else's data.

With this real-world analog, we can explore how blockchain works. The aforementioned qualities of entry validation by peer concurrence, real-time simultaneous updating, overruling of faulty records, and decentralization are all key attributes of blockchain. However, blockchain is digital and operates on a global scale so let's draw some analogies: the shoppers' notebooks are analogous to the digital blockchain records stored on computers around the world, and the grocery store is analogous to the entire globe.

The "blocks" in blockchain are groups of valid transactions. Each time a new valid transaction occurs, it's encrypted and linked to the previous block. This creates a chain of blocks, which is really just a sequence of records or transactions.

Similar to the grocery store example, public blockchains allow everybody on the system to see others' transactions, and this transparency is vital to security. Security and reliability also come from the blockchain system's encryption, which is done using math problems. Each new record is encrypted when it's added. Thus, when the lady behind you bought her $30 of gummy bears, blockchain would have used a difficult math problem to encrypt the entry and make it very difficult to change. These math problems are easy for a computer to solve and encrypt, but extremely difficult to reverse-engineer and unveil encrypted data.

So why all the hype about blockchain if it's just a way of writing down records? There are a few reasons it's being viewed as revolutionary:

1) **There's no central authority**. The records are shared and distributed across the world and stored on private computers, which means that no single authority can tamper with or censor data. Notice of new records are sent to all computers, and each computer will update its copy of the records to reflect the new transaction.

2) **Safety**. Any new record must be agreed upon before it's recorded. When a new record is approved, it's encrypted and linked back to the previous set of records. Additionally, since the entire system is shared among many people, there's no central repository or server storing the data. This

makes hacking much more difficult since there's no central point of vulnerability.

3) **Enhanced transparency**. The blockchain records are shared amongst everybody in the network. These shared records are only updated through consensus. Since everybody must agree on the updates, blockchain increases accuracy. The blockchain is visible to anybody with permission. Everybody has the same information, which increases trust.

4) **Increased efficiency**. All records are recorded in digital format so there's no need for paper. Also, since all new records are added to the existing records, only one blockchain is present. This eliminates the need to amalgamate or reconcile multiple documents.

5) **Increased traceability**. Recording records in blockchain provides a trail that can be both verified and audited. This is especially useful in supply chain logistics and financial services. Records of product shipments or transactions can be reliably traced backwards to verify authenticity or detect fraud.

You can think of blockchain as an infrastructure of sorts. Blockchain itself is just a way of keeping records, but the distributed nature, safety, speed and reliability of the technology opens many doors for truly revolutionary technologies and systems to arise.

I'm sure you can now see why blockchain is vital to the invention of digital currencies. Digital currencies are backed by nothing tangible, so your only proof of ownership is your digital wallet. Tampering of cryptocurrency data would be catastrophic, as millions or billions of dollars could potentially be wiped out with no means of recourse. Thus, no cryptocurrency would be possible without a reliable and safe process of affirming the authenticity of account balances and transactions.

Misc Topic 2: Cryptocurrency

Status of the technology: Proven technology. Cryptocurrencies are being traded around the world.

What to expect: Expect consolidation. There are an enormous number of experimental cryptocurrencies on the market but it's likely that many of the smaller currencies will go extinct in the next few years. Also expect governments to get involved – they're furious at the thought of full-grown adults responsibly exchanging goods and services with one another without their transactions being taxed.

Cryptocurrency is a polarizing topic. Proponents believe the technology will revolutionize trade, provide more secure transactions, upend the millennia-old practice of government-issued currencies, and give more bargaining power to individuals. Opponents have called it a Ponzi scheme, pyramid scheme, economic bubble, fad, and vehicle for money laundering, just to name a few.

Stipulations for what qualifies as a cryptocurrency vary, but in general it must meet at least these three key criteria:

1) No central authority. No government or issuing body oversees the currency.
2) The system defines how, whether, and when new currency is created. Expectations are delineated at the outset. This prevents unforeseen inflation or deflation events due to change in supply.
3) Ownership of cryptocurrency can be proved exclusively through cryptography. Cryptocurrencies are digital so there's no tangible or physical method to prove ownership.

Here we'll focus on Bitcoin since it's the first cryptocurrency and the most well-known. However, most cryptocurrencies work in a similar manner so most of what's discussed here can be generalized to all cryptocurrencies.

Supply and demand are the main drivers of the value of Bitcoin. The intrinsic value of the currency is solely determined by how much investors are willing to pay for them. This contrasts with most hard money in circulation today, which include commodity-backed money such as gold-backed currencies as well as fiat currencies, whose value is mostly determined by the monetary and fiscal policies of the issuing body. A Bitcoin is worth as much as the community is willing to pay for it. Simple as that. Recently, developers have been toying with backing or pegging cryptocurrencies to real-world assets but this is the exception rather than the norm.

Bitcoin supply is capped at 21 million coins, much like the way the supply of gold is capped on earth. Presently, Bitcoin is constantly being produced but by around 2140 the supply should reach 21 million and no more units will be created. This cap protects Bitcoin from mirroring the mass deflations that can occur when governments print huge sums of money. Thus in the 2100's, it's possible that Bitcoin could serve as a virtual commodity that could act as a hedge against inflation of traditional currencies, much like a virtual version of owning precious metals.

To own and trade Bitcoin, you would first need to acquire a digital Bitcoin wallet that contains encryption keys. Your public key is given to a buyer to receive payments, whereas your private key is used to send payments to others and to prove ownership of your wallet. You don't actually own the currency in your wallet or on your computer. Instead, your proof of ownership is stored throughout the world and maintained wherever the blockchain is maintained.

For every transaction, you announce the following to the bitcoin network:

1) your account number
2) receiver's account number
3) how many bitcoins are being sent

Once this "announcement" is made, the transaction will be processed by the distributed network of computers, not a central payment processor like Visa or Mastercard. The network of computers record the sender's information, receiver's information, and amount transferred, and enters the information to the end of the blockchain record. Each transaction is encrypted and must be verified by multiple points in the network. The verification process, performed by bitcoin miners, is computationally and energetically expensive. The miners are rewarded for expending electricity by receiving bitcoins for their services. Thus private computers around the world support the system. Transaction fees are low since bitcoin miners are rewarded and incentivized to contribute to processing the network.

The blockchain records every bitcoin transaction that has ever happened. When you're sending somebody bitcoins, you're not sending them files. Instead, you're telling everybody in the network to make a record of the transaction.

Reasons for the hype around cryptocurrencies include either perceived corporate or governmental subterfuge or simply a general mistrust of banks and governments. The runaway inflation in countries like Zimbabwe and Venezuela has some people looking to alternative assets whose value isn't at the mercy of the government. These people may have more faith in the long-term stability of cryptocurrencies due to security of the blockchain and the fact that coins are limited in number, which would theoretically prevent massive deflation.

Another reason for the hype is the partial anonymity. Though the transactions are public, your bitcoin address is all other people can see. The relative anonymity of transactions has made cryptocurrencies popular for money laundering and in the drug and weapons trades. Predictably, governments and regulators have been quick to demonize the currency on these grounds.

Yet another reason for the hype is that some people see cryptocurrencies as an investment. They can be traded for fiat currencies, and some people expect the price of the coins to rise in the future. However, since most cryptocurrencies are not backed by any real assets or any governmental entity, if the entire system or exchange collapses cryptocurrency investors could lose everything overnight. However, if derivatives trading has taught us anything, it's that there's no shortage of people with a substantial appetite for risk that are willing to invest in such volatile assets for higher potential returns.

Ironically, as cryptocurrencies gain popularity, governments will jump in to regulate them, which defeats the original purpose of the currency which was to get the government out. Of course, governments are salivating at the thought of taxing cryptocurrencies. Right now, cryptocurrency tax law is in its infancy, but tax guidelines (at least the Internal Revenue Service in the United States) indicate that they are to be treated not as currency, but as property like real estate or stocks and are subject to capital gains tax. Since the currency is constantly fluctuating in value as people are making transactions throughout the year, taxes become extremely difficult to calculate. Surely cryptocurrency tax law will mature from its current state.

<u>Misc Topic 3: Swarm robotics</u>

Status of the technology: In the initial stages of building robots that work together as one unified entity. Improvements are slow yet consistent. Computer algorithms based on swarming are finding more success currently.

What to expect: We can expect to see swarming robots doing jobs like construction in the future, possibly around the year 2050. Computer algorithms based on swarming principles are in effect now and will likely increase in use for logistics purposes because they can be used on massive datasets that would bog down traditional algorithms.

Schools of fish, herds of livestock, flocks of birds and colonies of ants are all made of a bunch of individual organisms that can move together in sync and act as one collective entity. Such collective behavior where no one organism is in charge and making the decisions is called swarming. Collectively swarms can accomplish great things, for instance tiny ¼ inch-long termites can create a termite mound that reaches 10 feet tall. Swarming is a type of **emergent behavior**, which typifies the common phrase "greater than the sum of its parts".

Swarming is a topic of research in manifold disciplines, most notably robotics. Swarm robotics is the subfield of robotics that seeks to program machines to exhibit swarming behavior. The ultimate goal of swarm robotics is **emergence**: the creation of complex global behaviors from the cooperation of many simple, noisy, and even error-prone robots following simple rules.

Designing each individual robot to be as simple as possible isn't simply cost-cutting or seeking a minimum viable model; it's intrinsic to swarming. To swarm, each organism or robot must put the collective before itself. Humans don't exhibit swarming behavior because our programming is too complex. We put ourselves first rather than the collective. For instance, humans will naturally attempt to minimize his or her own drive time to work rather than to drive in a manner that will minimize overall collective time wasted in a traffic jam. For example, some people will weave in and out of traffic to decrease his or her own personal drive time, but these actions can cause the braking of other cars which decreases the efficiency of the system as a whole.

For many researchers, ants serve as the archetypical swarming organism. The rules for ants are quite simple and are as follows. Ants initially wander around randomly to forage for food. Upon finding food, they grab some and drop a pheromone trail as they return to the nest. Any ant who doesn't know what to do will follow a nearby pheromone trail. By following and dropping these pheromone trails, eventually pheromone paths to the food will form. Any outgoing ants must yield to incoming ants, since the incoming ants are usually carrying food and are less maneuverable. This creates 3 lanes. Incoming ants will be in the middle and outgoing ants can yield to either the left or the right of the incoming ants, which creates two outside lanes.

Initially there may be several paths to a particular food source. The ants that find a shortest route end up going back and forth to the nest more often than the ants taking the longer route. A key property of pheromones is that they evaporate quickly, so ants must constantly travel down a path to keep the pheromone concentrations high. The pheromone trails become denser on the shorter paths which causes more ants to take that path. Eventually the ants converge on the shortest path due to reinforcement by pheromones. Each ant follows simple rules and is only concerned with its immediate local environment to decide what it will do next, but the colony as a whole exhibits emergent behavior that efficiently hones in on food sources.

Scientists have mimicked this foraging behavior to develop **the Ant Colony Optimization Algorithm**, which simulates foraging ants to optimize logistics using less computing power than conventional brute force computational methods. The algorithm is capable of finding the optimal routes for a fleet of delivery vehicles or finding the most efficient routes to direct internet traffic. As an example, let's say that a delivery service has 5,000 packages to deliver and 30 delivery trucks in the fleet. If you have a background in probability or statistics, you likely know how quickly increasing the number of combinations can cause the number of potential solutions to grow to truly astronomical numbers. Using brute force to calculate the best routes to deliver these 5,000 packages is a task that would give even a supercomputer a run for its money. The Ant Colony Optimization Algorithm that simulates the routes that ants take when foraging for food can be used in this scenario to "discover" the best series of routes for the trucks. The algorithm tests and reinforces the shorter paths that it finds rather than brute forcing every possible path. Thus, it requires much less computing power by foregoing calculating paths that are obviously inefficient. As the shorter paths are reinforced, longer paths lose strength. The overall solution is found by finding a series of optimal local solutions, much like swarming animals that are only concerned with themselves and their neighbors, rather than the entire swarm as a whole.

There's also a bee algorithm and other various swarming algorithms which can be used to find the most efficient way to solve complicated problems with billions, trillions, or even more possible solutions. On the whole, these typically function in a similar way as the ant algorithm.

Now back to physical robots rather than algorithms. A successful robot swarm would consist of individual robots that must necessarily be only concerned with themselves and those immediately around it, not what all the other robots in the collective are doing. They must be reactive, meaning the decisions must be made by the robot itself rather than by a central planner or brain. Scientists are on the cusp of creating such robots, so many applications will soon become available.

One important application is traffic. Ants and schooling fish don't get into traffic jams, and if we can get car traffic to similarly swarm it'll be much more efficient than the current process. Human-directed traffic is very inefficient, but if we implement swarming algorithms into self-driving cars, future commutes in the era of autonomous vehicles would be far more efficient than modern-day commutes.

Other applications are construction and search and rescue. Many small robots could be used to collectively dig or lay bricks, and swarming robots could be sent out into rubble after a natural disaster to look for people in rubble or otherwise in need.

Misc Topic 4: Railguns

Status of the technology: Proven technology.   Full-scale prototypes have been built.

What to expect: Advances in materials technology to address gun durability will be a necessity for economically sound large-scale implementation.

Electromagnetic railguns are ubiquitous in science fiction and video games set in the future. They're effectively giant cannons whose propulsive energy comes from electricity rather than chemical propellants like gunpowder, and the destructive power comes purely from kinetic energy from the speed of the projectile rather than from explosives. Railguns are no longer science fiction; they're science.

Railguns consist of three parts: the power source, a pail of parallel highly conductive metal rails, and an armature formed from several metallic, sliding conductors that house the projectile. To fire, millions of watts of power is released into one rail. The current travels up the rail, through the armature and down the other rail. The armature connects the two rails, completes the circuit, and essentially short circuits them.

The math is complex and beyond the scope here. It involves electrical right-hand-rules and a property known as the Lorentz force, which dictates the forces acting on an object that is simultaneously under magnetic and electric fields. The result of the electrical pulse is a combined electric and magnetic field that imparts a huge force acting parallel to the rails that sends the armature down the barrel. The armature segments fall away after the projectile leaves the barrel.

Railguns are not difficult to make. You can make a miniature railgun in a single afternoon in your kitchen with items from a hardware store. The problem is scaling the system up to weaponize it. As the technology is scaled up from kitchen-sized to military grade, several problems arise.

The first issue is power. As an example, the United States' prototype electromagnetic railgun is the country's most powerful cannon that can shoot projectiles at 7 to 8 times the speed of sound, but operating it requires enough electricity to power around 19,000 homes. This severely restricts the logistics and flexibility of the gun. The U.S. Zumwalt-class destroyers are some of the only ships in existence capable of generating the 25 megawatts needed to operate a railgun while also maintaining the ship's base electrical needs.

The second issue is durability. The rails warp, melt, and try to actively tear themselves apart each time a projectile is fired. The force that propels the armature forward also acts to push the rails apart, so they must be heavily reinforced. As of now, the rails need to be replaced after only a few shots. Finding a conductive material capable of withstanding the incredible wattage and friction to use for the rails is an active area of research in materials science. It will take a breakthrough in materials science to develop rails than can withstand more than a few shots before needing to be replaced.

So why are militaries researching railguns in the first place? Don't missiles have superior range and accuracy? The answer to this question is that the railgun fills a specific niche that complements current technologies and has certain benefits:

1) There are still some benefits to dumb projectiles. Missiles can be spoofed, jammed, intercepted and hacked, but a railgun projectile can't.
2) The railgun is superior to current generation gunpowder cannons because the projectiles can be fired around 5,700 miles per hour, which is several times the velocity of typical gunpowder rounds. These projectiles are much more difficult to dodge compared to traditional projectiles going only a few hundred miles per hour.

3) The projectiles are very cheap compared to missiles or higher-technology rounds. If the aforementioned durability issue can be resolved, the railgun would be a very economical weapon.

These immediate technical hurdles, most notably the durability issue, hasn't stopped NASA and other groups from speculating and proposing wild uses for railgun technology. Various methods of launching spacecraft into orbit using a railgun have been proposed, most notably the launch of a scramjet. Scramjets engines require supersonic flow to work properly, so a railgun could theoretically fire a scramjet into the sky at several times the speed of sound, and the engine would power itself the rest of the way towards orbit and launch payloads into space. Cool idea, but this wouldn't be realized for many years to come.

The scramjet idea is only one idea of many. Railguns and variants on railgun technology are very popular in the non-rocket spacelaunch community. Electromagnetic catapults and other electromagnetic launch systems have been proposed as alternatives to the launch loop or space elevator (both entries in this book) to get payloads to space at a lower price than traditional chemical rocketry.

<u>Misc Topic 5: Augmented Reality</u>

Status of the technology: It's here. Pokémon Go, Snapchat filters, weather forecasting...

What to expect: Expect numerous applications to be rolled out in the very near future. Many current applications today are focused on sports and leisure, but we can expect to see many upcoming applications in professional fields.

The goal of augmented reality is to alter a person's perception of physical reality. Objects that reside in the real world are enhanced by computer-generated information that can change the way you feel, smell, see, or hear. The goal is to blend the digital and real world or to enhance the real world. It seeks to offer enriched experiences over what reality can offer. Various types of equipment can display augmented reality, including headsets, smart glasses, phones, and televisions. Future technologies seek to display augmented reality on smart contacts lenses or directly into the eye via virtual retinal display.

Some types of augmented reality have already been implemented:

1) Weather forecasting. Digital images are overlaid on the screen with the real world caster.
2) The digital first down line in American Football or digital sponsors being overlaid on the ground in other sports.
3) Snapchat filters. Animals, accessories, makeup, and other effects are superimposed onto real world pictures or video.
4) For anyone who joined in the fad in 2016, Pokémon Go is another application of augmented reality. The digital monsters were incorporated into the real world.

This technology will see many more applications in the coming years. The following is a quick list of what we might see:

1) Healthcare – A system that detects veins below the surface and projects an image of them onto the surface of the skin to make inserting a needle easier.
2) Healthcare – Simulated surgery training for new healthcare professionals.
3) Psychology - Treating certain phobias such as spiders and roaches by gradually "introducing" them to the patient in the real world.
4) Glasses that can provide a heads-up-display which can provide time, calendar, health information, pictures, and data in your regular field of vision
5) More immersive flight simulations and training
6) Military training and simulated battles
7) Advanced vehicle navigation overlaying upcoming turns or mile markers into your field of vision
8) Tourism – glasses or a headset could provide information about what the tourist is looking at
9) Real-time translation of documents in another language. A person's native language could be displayed over the foreign language to replace it.
10) Real-time translation of speech. Spoken words could be displayed as subtitles in your native language in your field of view.

The technology typically utilizes cameras, sensors, accelerometers, gyroscopes, and possibly GPS to gather information. The program processes the information by using simultaneous localization and mapping. That is, the program creates and constantly updates a map while simultaneously keeping track of where the person/device is inside this map. Once the data has been processed, the program will provide the appropriate output that will add a digital layer of information to the user's reality.

Augmented reality doesn't involve closing yourself off from the outside world. Instead, it seeks to enhance the real world that you're experiencing. This is a key difference between this technology and virtual reality, the technology discussed in the next entry.

<u>Misc Topic 6: Virtual Reality</u>

Status of the technology: Virtual reality games and simulations are here, but they're not sophisticated enough to fully simulate reality. Frame rate lag causes headaches in a large percentage of users.

What to expect: Virtual reality will continue to improve as computers improve. Higher processing and frame rates will likely be a necessity before the rollout of any applications other than novelty demonstrations. We might reasonably expect to see useful virtual reality applications by 2030 or 2035.

In **virtual reality**, the user's experience is completely based on virtual information. This contrasts with augmented reality, where the user experiences a blend of real-world information and virtual information.

While various projecting technologies can be used for virtual reality, the most popular current setup is a headset that can track the user's head and eye movements and includes a fully 3D and stereoscopic display. This allows the display to change with the user's perspective. Separate projections for each eye creates stereoscopic vision and a sense of 3 dimensions, and a built in gyroscope senses when the goggles move. The headset will fully immerse the person into a simulated world, and the person can move and look around the virtual space.

A person's peripheral vision in the real world will limit how deeply he or she is immersed in the virtual world, thus the helmet needs to be fully enclosed to enter full virtual reality. As an example, think of standard currently available first-person shooter video games on the market. The person is role-playing as the character in the game, but the gamer's peripheral vision in the real world limits the person from fully immersing himself into the game.   Closing off these peripherals with a full virtual reality headset heightens the experience and the person more closely feels as if the game is real.

Virtual reality is still mostly in its infancy. An insufficiently high frame rate causes headaches for many people wearing the headset. The person is intended to believe that the virtual world is real, but the choppiness and few milliseconds of lag time between the user's movements and the display response creates a mis-match between the user's eyes and his or her brain, leading to what has been termed "virtual reality sickness".   The sickness has similar symptoms to motion sickness, which in addition to the headache can include nausea, vomiting, fatigue, and disorientation.

The ultimate goal of virtual reality is termed **simulated reality**, which is so immersive that it's indistinguishable from reality and the user no longer knows if the reality is simulated or real. In the near term, however, projected applications for virtual reality somewhat parallel those of augmented reality, such as use in driving schools, medical schools, or phobia treatment.

Augmented and virtual reality often aren't fully interchangeable in their applications; instead, they can compliment one another. For instance, virtual reality can be used in architecture and real estate to simulate a walkthrough of a proposed new house that hasn't been built yet. On the contrary, augmented reality can be used when walking through an actual house, with the internal piping or electrical wires superimposed on the real-life view.

Misc Topic 7: Graphene

Status of the technology: Powdered graphene can be produced at scale, but wide sheets are much more expensive and difficult to produce. Graphene sheets must be a single atom layer thick, which is proving to be a manufacturing challenge.

What to expect: Applications containing powdered graphene are on the market now. Most futuristic applications of graphene generally rely on the material's electrical conductive properties which only arise when graphene is produced as a large sheet rather than a powder. We can expect these applications to be rolled out concomitantly with advances in manufacturing, perhaps around 2035.

Graphene is a substance made of a one atom thick layer of carbon atoms that are arranged in tessellated hexagons, much like chicken-wire or honeycomb. From this geometry, unique and exotic properties emerge. For its thickness, it's 100 times stronger than steel and it carries electricity more quickly, precisely, and efficiently than any other known material. It's also the most impermeable material discovered to date. Electrons can move across graphene with virtually zero resistance, and this incredible electrical conductivity could make the material an eventual replacement for silicon in microchips. Electrons move faster across graphene than they can in silica, and they're also subjected to less disruption since graphene is smoother and the electrons can take a straight path across the graphene since it has few flaws in the microstructure if manufactured properly.

In the mid-2000's international media was abuzz with speculations on the potential applications of graphene, from bionic humans to glowing wallpaper to space elevators. Now we don't hear much about graphene anymore. What happened?

The short answer is that these applications are still coming, they'll just take time. The biggest problem facing graphene-based applications right now is economics. Graphene is still difficult and expensive to produce commercially. The material must not only be one atom thick for its electrical and conductive properties to manifest, but it must also be a minimum of several centimeters across for most applications. It loses its attractive properties and becomes graphite if it's made thicker than one or two atoms. Though large sheets are still difficult to manufacture, graphene powder is now being produced in large quantities due to its heat conductive properties and its incredibly low weight-to-volume ratio.

We can draw an analogy between our current grasp on graphene manufacturing with that of the early days of silicon manufacturing. In the 1960's silicon was also very expensive to produce, but the future economic potential of the material resulted in a significant amount of time and money being dumped into developing production methods that brought the price down several orders of magnitude. We're already seeing a similar drop in the price of graphene but it's not cheap enough to be economically viable on a large scale just yet. The European Union has already invested over a billion dollars in research grants that will support graphene research into the mid 2020's.

One hurdle to graphene replacing silicon in electronics is that it's better, but not better enough. A technology must be truly transformative to replace such well-established, mature technology in any reasonable amount of time. It may take a few decades for graphene to reasonably supplant silicon in electronics since silicon is already well-researched and silicon manufacturing methods have been honed and mastered over the past few decades.

The following is a list of graphene-containing products already on the market and the benefit that graphene adds to the product:

- Watch – weight reduction
- Earbuds – weight reduction and flexibility

- Fishing rods – strength and flexibility
- Ski jackets – heat conductive, antibacterial, and drag reducing properties
- Solid State Drive for memory storage – heat dissipation and thermal cooling
- Bicycle wheels – increase in heat dissipation, puncture resistance, and stiffness.
- Bicycle frame – weight reduction
- Bicycle helmet – weight reduction, impact absorption

As these examples suggest, many currently available products on the market containing graphene take advantage of the low density of powdered graphene for cutting weight as well as the heat conductivity properties. This contrasts with the media-hyped futuristic applications of graphene, which are nearly all based on graphene's ability to transfer electric current. The large, thin sheets of graphene necessary for these technologies must be free of flaws and are much more difficult to produce than raw graphene powder.

In the medium term, we can expect graphene sheets to be used in products like touchscreens, which would be more responsive, less brittle, and cheaper than current screens. Most current screens require indium, which is a rare and expensive element. Thus, as indium becomes increasingly expensive to procure, this would create a perfect opportunity for touchscreen manufacturers to pilot novel graphene technology. Using graphene sheets, we can also expect faster charging, more energy dense, and longer lasting batteries and supercapacitors.

In sum, here is what we can expect out of graphene:

1) Current/near term -- Graphene powder incorporated into products to decrease weight and increase flexibility and heat conductive properties across many industries.

2) Medium term – Improvements to current technologies such as computers, solar panels, touchscreens and batteries.
3) Long term – Glowing wallpaper, flexible wearable biosensors, ultralight aircraft, the sky is the limit

I'll leave you with a joke.
Q: Is there anything graphene can't do?
A: It can't get out of the lab.